Victims

It's Not Natural After All

Tim G. Riley

For God is my witness, whom I serve with my spirit in the gospel of His Son, that without ceasing I make mention of you always in my prayers, making request if, by some means, now at last I may find a way in the will of God to come to you. For I long to see you, that I may impart to some spiritual gift, so that you may be established. Romans 1.9-11

Disclaimer:
The people, websites and other documentation that are referenced in this publication in no manner, way or form endorse the contents of this independent writing. The references appear for the reader's individual verification, and those sources may alter the presentation of information from the time of this writing. Professionals and sources may possess licenses to serve people in methods other than are included or excluded in this writing; therefore, principles in this writing in no manner, way or form replace professional service for people whom require professional service or their previous service. The contents of this writing in no manner, way or form intend animosities; therefore, people who draw conclusions from this writing's intent may disregard subjective interpretations and contrary nuances of words that are other than innocuous in nature. Garland Logos, LLC and its representation are not responsible for misinterpretation, unauthorized use and (or) misuse of the contents of this writing.

Garland Logos, LLC's chief manager and president is Timothy G. Riley.

Copyright © 2010 Tim G. Riley
All rights reserved.

ISBN: 1-4515-3254-7
ISBN-13: 9781451532548

dedication: To victims of premature exposure to adult sexual subjects.

CONTENTS

About the Author	vii
Sincere Gratitude	ix
Forward	xi
PART I:	
THE CREATOR'S MEANING OF LIFE IN THE US CONSTITUTION	1
Chapter One: Preaching the Forbidden Fruit to the Choir	3
Chapter Two: Understood Invisible Things	11
Chapter Three: The Origin Indicates the Outcome	17
PART II:	
THE CREATOR'S MEANING OF LIBERTY IN THE US CONSTITUTION	29
Chapter Four: The Outcome Indicates the Origin	31
Chapter Five: Constitutional Cultures and Subcultures	43
Chapter Six: Above Compound English's Nomenclature	55
PART III:	
THE CREATOR'S MEANING OF THE PURSUIT OF HAPPINESS IN THE US CONSTITUTION	63
Chapter Seven: Beyond Defensive to Proactive	65
Chapter Eight: Axiomatic Laws of Nature and Nature's God	77
Chapter Nine: Deliverance From Evil on Three Strategic Fronts	89
Proverbs: People's Perception of Priorities	99
A collection of Proverbs from this writing for your reference .	
Notes:	101

about the author: As a husband, father and grandfather—God's inspired Tim G. Riley to expound the Founding Fathers' foundation for legislation to preserve our posterity's perception. Was the Founding Fathers' foresight inspired through the glimmer of hope in a child's eye?

He's advocated for the expulsion of an unnatural and transient philosophy from compulsory as well as post-secondary education. He's persistently written letters to newspapers, politicians and education administrators including the US Department of Education.

The author honestly maintains that the *Declaration of Independence's* centrist perception most often exemplifies the Christian creed. Even though, the mass media often labels a Christian view "right wing."

With the publication of VICTIMS, he continues to advocate for the protection of our posterity's natural and innocent perception. *VICTIMS—IT'S NOT NATURAL AFTER ALL* expounds our Constitutional rights with divine providence and without prejudice.

sincere gratitude: My gratitude goes to my Heavenly Father who works in the hearts of people when thinking of teachers of the Bible. Contemplating the accomplishment of Jesus Christ our Savior who makes intercession for all of the saints continues to inspire me.

My appreciation to my wife who shares my love for God and family. The perspective that she shares concerning life assists to complete me as God intended.

To the dedicated Sisters of the Order of Saint Benedict, thank-you sincerely . Affectionately referred to as "the nuns," they prayed, taught and fought for more souls of children than any other group to my knowledge during the 60s.

When faced with adversity, I asked God for something positive in my life. God directed me to a second-hand paperback book titled *The Power of Positive Thinking*. Thankfully, the late, Dr. Norman Vincent Peale's labor of love lives in people's hearts—especially mine.

To God's glory, Dr. Pat Robertson's dedication to keep Christians comprehensively informed has been exemplary. The Christian Broadcasting Network's *700 Club* has provided impartial news of current events that is vital to preserve freedom. The *700 Club's* up-to-date reporting has inspired me to expound the self-evident facts and truths in this writing to inspire others, also.

My thanks to you (the reader) that your adventure with God may be more enriched from your reading of *VICTIMS*.

forward: A child's perspective is priceless. It's full of wonder. This writing humbly presents that a child comprehends an innocuous perception of life, liberty and the pursuit of happiness. It's axiomatic that the Founding Fathers' labor of love in the *US Constitution* protects our posterity's perspective. It's inspirational that we live in the Country that protects human rights.

Through God's grace, practical information is available from the Bible. Similarly, the *Declaration of Independence* or the *Constitution of the United States* is an authoritative resource for practical information. The Internet also offers some reliable resources including .gov statistical websites.

You, the reader, may expect three things from this writing. God always gets the glory as the Bible states in Ephesians 2:9: *Not of works, lest anyone should boast.* An immoral issue has a godly and political solution. Your unique contribution as a citizen really does make a difference.

A pertinent statistic's relevance requires consideration in direct proportion to the nature of the organization providing the statistic. For example, a sexually oriented organization presents partial statistics to corroborate its organization's perceived, political position. That's tangible. Statistical analysis needs to consider impartiality as the first guideline for a meaningful statistic.

A religious organization more often than not provides an impartial statistic in accordance with the *US Constitution*. A Constitutional organization's nature utilizes provident consideration that ultimately benefits all people regardless of race, color, creed or national origin. It's no coincidence that Revelations 5.9 reads: *And they sang a new song saying: "You are worthy to take the scroll, and to open its seals. For You were slain, and have redeemed us to God by Your blood. Out of every tribe and tongue and nation and people."*

Blindly trusting that an organization is beneficial without identifying its nature is like going to a well without water. 2 Peter 2.17: *These are wells without water, clouds carried by a tempest, for whom is reserved the blackness of darkness forever.* The innocuous pursuit of happiness exemplifies the Laws of Nature and Nature's God. History is full of disastrous trial and error experiments. When the test subject is a human guinea pig, no prejudice exists when assigning destructive labels to such barbarous acts. Then, why has an institution like public education ignored prudence?

Self-evident practices don't need statistics to support a concept like Constitutional freedom. In principle, business and government institutions need to adopt tangible policies and procedures. Today, organizations deny tangible results to embrace the intangible. The groups speculate that the experiment is going to be successful at the expense of others (often children).

The primary Bible references, included in this writing, are from the New King James Version (NKJV). The King James Version (KJV) and New King James Version are identified with their appropriate acronym when referenced in close proximity to each other, or KJV is noted when it's the only scripture reference. Both, the NKJV and KJV italicize English words that do not have a corresponding Greek word with the exception of some quotes in the NKJV. Because the scriptures in this writing are italicized, the added words are not italicized. So that, you (the reader) are able to recognize a word without a corresponding Greek word. Occurrences of the italicized words are frequently helpful for understanding the Bible.

PART 1
THE CREATOR'S MEANING OF LIFE IN THE US CONSTITUTION

Precious words from a child's perspective: "Where we live, the Cr'ater gives us nat'ral rights that are in the 'Stitution (US Constitution). Oh—and, it's not 'structive (destructive) 'cause the first, big gift is Life."

Chapter 1
Preaching the Forbidden Fruit to the Choir

It is axiomatic that a child knows the value of a loving parent-child relationship. Uncomplicated, a child makes a request from a parent with the high expectation for an answer. That's why Jesus thought so highly of a child's attitude.

What does it really mean to be converted? Matthew 18.3: *And said, "Assuredly, I say to you, unless you are converted and become as little children, you will by no means enter the kingdom of heaven."* A sound foundation exists for those who believe the saying, "There's no such thing as a bad child." From God's perspective, there isn't. Because God is the Heavenly Father, He knows what His child needs. This perspective is one of many reasons that the family unit is so vital. How a child approaches a parent to request assistance is a living example. That's how an adult needs to approach a relationship with the Heavenly Father.

The concept of "lordship" is quite frequently misunderstood in our American culture. A working relationship between a master and an apprentice is a traditional parallel. A more modern analogy is the mentoring relationship between an intern with a professional. For example, an intern needs to confirm the plan of action with the professional before carrying out the task for the head of the organization and the company. An intern actively seeks professional advice during the entire internship.

It's important to recognize that the Jewish creed's perspective of lordship still considers a person without Hebrew ancestry a Gentile. However without prejudice, the Lord Jesus restores a family relationship for each person whom believes. The Word of God reveals the same in Ephesians 2.19: *Now, therefore, you are no longer strangers and foreigners, but fellow citizens with the saints and members of the household of God.* Hebrews 8.10 documents the epitome of Jesus' lordship and follows: *"For this is the covenant that I will make with the house of Israel after those days says the Lord: I will put My laws in their mind and write them on their hearts; and I will be their God, and they shall be My people."* Jesus' initial lordship is exclusive between God and a believer as the following verse Hebrews 8.11 confirms: *"None of them shall teach his neighbor, and none his brother, saying, 'Know the Lord,' for all shall know Me, from the least of them to the greatest of them."* Although, enhancing or enriching Jesus' lordship increases with the nurture or admonition of the Lord. What an amazing redemption! You may now retain God's Word in your mind.

Retention of God's Word was limited before Christ. After God raised Jesus from the dead, salvation was first declared to Jewish descendants and follows in Acts 2.36: *"God had made this Jesus, whom you crucified, both Lord and Christ."* With this in mind, this is when some Hebrew people repented and were baptized in the name of Jesus Christ for the remission of sins and received the gift of the Holy Spirit.

God expresses that it is important to remember that Jesus is our peace between the Jewish creed and Gentile creed. Ephesians 2.14 reads: *For He Himself is our peace, who has made both one, and has broken down the middle wall of separation.* Before Christ's redemption, the Jewish creed's belief expounds that Abraham's seed is exclusive to God's blessing. Abraham's seed now includes all of those who walk in the faith of Abraham. The understanding of Abraham's seed is available with Christ. Without overemphasis, peace's foundation resides in Christ. Regardless of one's ancestry as a child in God's family, you have peace in Christ and with one another.

A nation is at peace when a nation is not at odds with another nation. But, peace is commonly thought to be a state of mental attitude, and it is when it is Christ's peace within God's family. Jesus' response explains peace to a question from a disciple in John 14.27: *Peace I leave with you, My peace I give to you; not as the world gives do I give to you. Let not your heart be troubled, neither let it be afraid.* The world has a totally different idea of peace. So, peace is also a state of mental well-being.

In Genesis, humankind originally was at peace with God. God provided peace and safety to them with the tree of life. No apparent need for a Messiah existed without understanding that Adam and Eve questioned God's peace and safety because they took and ate the fruit from the tree of knowledge of good and evil. God has constantly looked-out for the well-being of His children. Timeless—just like then, now, the serpent has contradicted what God declared as peace and safety.

God outlines what is safe in the Bible. Currently, the meaning of safe is not being preserved. When peace is no longer God's definition of peace and safety is not God's safety, destruction is the result. The Bible states in 1 Thessalonians 5.3: *For when they say, "Peace and safety!" then sudden destruction comes upon them.* Each person who verbalizes this prophesy propagates synthetic peace and a false sense of safety.

The public sexual education curricula has contributed to the casual attitude towards sex. Education has been reaping the fruit of its labors. Sexual education has needed to admit to its contribution to America's despair natality statistics in order restore and not reform traditional education. Not reform, because education reform has a history of contriving instead of eliminating the same inordinate sexual education program. Forgiveness for public education's avarice has equal importance to the drastic change that is necessary for a limited program that refuses to prematurely expose children to adult sexual subjects.

Currently, a word of wisdom to live by has taken second-fiddle to the "it's all good" philosophy in public education. The unmarried status for parents that are currently having children has increased as recorded on the Nation Center for Health Statistics (NCHS) with the Center for Disease Control and Prevention's (CDC) www.cdc.gov/nchs/births.htm website and follows: "All measures of childbearing by unmarried women increased in the United States to historic levels in 2007 (preliminary data) (1.4). The total number of births to unmarried women increased 4 percent from 2006, to 1,714,643. The 2007 total is up 26 percent from 2002 when the recent steep increases began."

God included the following safe hierarchy in Genesis 1.26 that public education at one time embraced: *Then God said, "Let Us make man in Our image, according to Our likeness; let them have dominion over the fish of the sea, over the birds of the air, and over the cattle, over all the earth and over every creeping thing that creeps on the earth."* God gave humankind the authority to rule over all of the creatures and resources including the air, water and land. Today, this concept has been almost impossible for people to grasp because there are some ferocious creatures on earth. Nevertheless, God's order in nature to the creatures was initially respected by Adam and Eve. Just like God told Adam and Eve about natural activity, tending of the garden by Adam and Eve initially honored God's instructions and preserved creatures on earth.

In the animal kingdom, an order of dominance remains even today. An animal trainer assumes dominance at the top of the animal kingdom. But, a lion is the king of the jungle. An eagle rules the air. For the reason of sheer size, a whale dominates the sea." One common trait that any dominant creature has is that it's trainable including a human being. If a person makes time to watch an animal trainer, an audible command is often accompanied with body language. The body language of a trainer is equally important as an audible command. As a reader, you may probably agree that animal training principles are not at all common. If a vicious animal confronts you, it is advisable for you to ask God what to do like Daniel in the lions' den. Moreover, do not allow yourself to be placed in an awkward situation with a beast; unless, God specifically directs you.

The Laws of Nature and Nature's God include the blessings that God delivered to Adam and Eve. Genesis 1.28 reads: *Then God blessed them and God said to them, "Be fruitful and multiply; fill the earth; and subdue it; have dominion over the fish of the sea, over the birds of the air, and over every living thing that move on the earth."* God confirms humankind's dominion on earth. The Creator of humankind has the right to instruct people's utilization of their dominion. Not only does the Creator know how nature efficiently operates, the Creator's purpose needs to be understood. A deliberate decision needs to be made in order for humankind to follow the instructions.

In the beginning, people were designated as vegetarians on the food chain, and animals were herbivores. Genesis 2.16-17: *And the Lord God commanded the man, saying, "Of every tree of the garden you may freely eat; but of the tree of the knowledge of good and evil you shall not eat, for in the day you eat of it you shall surely die."* For good reason, God gave Adam and Eve specific dietary instructions. Of the fruit from every tree of the garden, humankind could freely eat but not the tree of knowledge of good and evil. Genesis 1.30: *Also, to every beast of the earth, to every bird of the air, and to every thing that creeps on the earth, in which* there is *life,* I have given *every herb for food; and it was so. In the garden of Eden, creatures were not carnivorous.*

You may have heard chapter three of Genesis taught. When the serpent omitted the word "freely" and substituted the word "not," the serpent was opposing Adam and Eve's freedom and dominion. Genesis 3.1: *Now the serpent was more cunning than any beast of the field which the Lord God had made. And he said to the woman,"Has God indeed said, 'You shall not eat of every tree of the garden?'"* Unnatural sustenance opposed God's dietary recommendations and defied the order in the garden. In considering the situation, the herbivore ought to have followed and not questioned the rules from God to Adam and Eve. The serpent was violating food safety protocols. Freedom to regulate the wide and healthy variety of food accompanied Adam and Eve's authority. Although, the free healthy choice was impaired in Genesis 3.6 and follows: *So when the woman saw the tree* was *good for food, that it* was *pleasant to the eyes, and a tree desirable to make* one *wise, she took of its fruit and ate. She also gave to her husband with her, and he ate.*

What was a serpent doing talking to a human? Exactly! Even, today's common sense has taught us to stay a good, safe distance away from a serpent. Practical safety has been one of the first rules of human nature since the beginning of time.

Humankind's duty was to maintain order over all of the creatures in the garden. Humankind's presence in the garden signified authority over the creatures. Eve was authorized to continue to dominate and not question God's peace and safety. The erratic behavior from the serpent was a reason for Eve to redirect the serpent because the serpent was trespassing among the trees in humankind's territory.

In congruence (in this once perfect world), a wildlife species mingled harmoniously with its own kind. God said in Genesis 1.25: *And God made the beast of the earth according to its kind, cattle according to its kind, and everything that creeps on the earth according to its kind. And God saw that it* was *good.* Eve knew that the serpent was supposed to mingle with its own kind. In the animal kingdom, God's blessing revolved around a creature mingling within its own kind. Even in today's corrupt world, a creature depending on its species has continued to heard, flock or school together with its own kind.

Adam and Eve's abuse of authority (bending the rules) altered their and every human being's heart, soul and mind. We all have been victims of Adam and Eve's abuse of authority. Our body, soul and spirit were at enmity with God, and we were embarrassed. Physical, mental and spiritual abuse required the Messiah for God's deliverance.

It has been suggested that the record of the "serpent" in Genesis is not actually about a serpent. It was a serpent as evidenced going forward. Genesis 3.14-15 reads, *So the Lord God said to the serpent: "Because you have done this, you* are *cursed more than all cattle, and more than every beast of the field. On your belly you shall go, and you shall eat dust all the days of your life. And I will put enmity between you and the woman, and between your seed and her Seed. He shall bruise your head, and you shall bruise His heel."* Not only was the serpent redirected to go on its belly, but the serpents dietary requirements were altered from herbs to dust even as today. God also revealed the consequences of Adam and Eve's evil choice. Moreover, God announced His plan to restore humankind.

People forfeit some of God's protection when they do not follow God's guidance. Proverbs 18.21: *Death and life* are *in the power of the tongue, and they that love it shall eat its fruit.* Digesting God's Word of life results in talking words of life. Proverbs 18.20: *A man's stomach shall be satisfied from the fruit of his mouth;* from *the produce of his mouth he shall be filled.*

God inspired Solomon to give us a glimpse of what the tree of life was in Proverbs 3.18 (speaking of God's wisdom and understanding): *She* is *a tree of life to those who take hold of her, and happy* are all *who retain her.* The Spirit (God) gives life. The tree of life bore the fruit of God's wisdom and understanding. God's tree of life was guarded from Adam and Eve, but the hope of Jesus opened the way to live forever. Jesus said in the gospel of John 6.63, *"It is the Spirit that gives life; the flesh profits nothing. The words that I speak to you are spirit, and they are life."* The tree of the knowledge of good and evil also bore words but of good and evil. Jesus explained that God's words are knowledge of life in Matthew 4.4: *But he answered and said, "It is written, 'Man shall not live by bread alone, but by every word that proceeds from the mouth of God.'"* God originated the idea of food for thought or mental diet.

Instead of magnifying God's wisdom, genius has been misappropriated like so many extraordinary ideas. Humankind's magnificence has been given the privilege of acknowledging God's precious gift of life but has wasted glory on fame and fortune. The fullness of life was experienced by Adam and Eve, but life with God was reconciled when Jesus (the Life) redeemed us.

Practical principles abound in the biblical record of Adam and Eve. We know in part because God's Spirit is in us. When Jesus returns for us, we will fully know about God. Our objectives as children of God are to enrich our relationships with God in our every day lives. Hebrews 1.1 reads: *God who at various times and in various ways spoke in time past to the fathers by the prophets, has in these last days spoken to us by His Son, whom He has appointed heir of all things, through whom also He made the worlds.*

God's foundational guidebook for raising children is the book of Proverbs. From Proverbs 1.7, *The fear* (acknowledgment of God's respectful omnipotence) *of the Lord* is *the beginning of knowledge.* Each child is so unique, so only God can supply universal knowledge that is true for all children. A person who acknowledges God concerning raising children receives the correct instructions to raise children as promised in Proverbs 3.5-6: *Trust in the Lord with all your heart, and lean not on your own understanding. In all your ways acknowledge Him, and He shall direct your paths.* A child-rearing method that can be substantiated from God's word has tremendous merit. A parent truly needs to ask God for guidance in unique situations. Any theory that universally works for children can be documented from the Bible. The Bible is our primary source for guidance.

Acknowledging God encompasses personal dedication including a person's heart, soul and mind. Matthew 22.37 states: *Jesus said to him, "You shall love the Lord your God with all your heart, with all your soul, and with all your mind."* God produces the fruit of the Spirit from a person's nurturing of God's Word as recorded in Galatians 5.22-23: *But the fruit of the Spirit is love, joy, peace, longsuffering, kindness, goodness, faithfulness, gentleness, self-control. Against such there is no law.* Prayer that honors God's sphere of influence results in action that fulfills God's plan as expounded in Ephesians 6.18: *Praying always with all prayer and supplication in the Spirit, being watchful to this end with all perseverance and supplication for all the saints.*

People that do not have applied knowledge of the truth are easily swayed by the drug-induced child psychology of the day. Please note, unmarried and homosexual parents need the knowledge of God's guidance for raising children. Because, non-traditional parents are one contributor short of God's order in a family relationship. Incomplete couples through grace still have access to God's guidebook of knowledge. To complicate matters when educators under-emphasize traditional marriage, chaos is the rule and is the determining factor in the confusion that occurs in the minds of the school-age children.

A child and natural parents together with God exemplify a godly relationship and are more than worth respecting and preserving. Three vital things need to be present for effectively raising children in the nurture and admonition of the Lord, a man, a woman and a godly defined marriage. Deviations from this properly aligned relationship are definitely a drawback (challenge) in raising children. Knowledge, understanding and wisdom from God for raising children enrich a married couple's relationship through reading the Bible and going to church together.

Because the divorce rate now exceeds fifty percent, a deviation from the Ecclesiastes 4.11 threefold cord needs special attention with God's guidance. God is able to compensate for the lack of one of the parent's presence. An important element in God's guidance is recorded in Proverbs 4.7: *Wisdom is the principal thing.* When a believer praises, thanks and acknowledges the Lord, God's supplies guidance concerning raising your children. God is love, so all of His guidance follows His order in life. One of the basic principles in life to expound for children is respect for life. Self respect for a believer means disciplining children with forgiveness, dignity and individuality. 2 Corinthians 2.11: *Lest Satan should take advantage of us; for we are ignorant of his devices.*

It is important take an inventory of God's rewards. To begin with, Psalms 127.3 reads, *Behold, children* are *a heritage from the Lord, the fruit of the womb* is a reward. Remember Jesus' perspective in Matthew 25.40: *"And the King will answer and say to them, 'Assuredly, I say to you, inasmuch as you did* it *to one of the least of these My brethren, you did* it *to Me.'"*

Chapter 2
Invisible Things—You Can't Prove That

One of the embarrassments of Adam and Eve's abuse of authority is homosexuality. In the event that you (the reader) are a victim of homosexual abuse, you are not alone. God works out a plan for every person's deliverance from sin's consequences.

God loves people, but God doesn't love homosexuality. Without prejudice, God makes a distinction between previous behavior and a victim's deliverance. In Hebrews 4.12, God expounds a victim's separation from ungodly behavior and follows: *For the Word of God is living and powerful, and sharper than any two-edged sword, piercing even to the division of soul and spirit, and of joints and marrow, and is a discerner of the thoughts and intents of the heart.* The overwhelming humiliation that a homosexual abuse victim experiences intimidates. God's Word is greater than previous behavior. Nurturing His promises gives a person a new perspective. Is the homosexual abuse even possible to repair? God's hope leaves old ways behind and embraces a new life.

The following scripture brought to remembrance an encounter with one such blessed young woman. Matthew 5.6: *Blessed* are *those who hunger and thirst for righteousness, for they shall be filled.* With nary a cloud in the sky, she sat on a bench looking hopelessly into space. Greeting her, I asked, "How may I be of assistance to you, today?" I shared that God was able to deliver a person in the most adverse situation. I listened genuinely and mentioned, "Did you know that many scriptures are specifically written with "you" in mind? Romans 10.9: *That if you confess with your mouth the Lord Jesus and believe in your heart that God has raised Him from the dead, you will be saved.* This scripture provides a personal answer to the question, "How am I saved?" Yes—God's word is that personal. From regular Bible study, "you" is a word that God quite often utilizes.

Something was askew with this thirsting soul, but I didn't press her for more details because I was at that time a stranger. God told me that she wasn't being completely candid. However for a first encounter, our conversation was quite extensive. Before parting, I gave her my address and telephone number just in case she ever had a need to talk.

For months, I saw her sitting in the same vicinity and greeted her waiting for her to reciprocate. But, she vehemently waved me away. Kind of like, her boyfriend was in close proximity. Enough was enough. One day, I sat down next to her and implored, "Please tell me what has been bothering you." She exclaimed, "It's hopeless. You don't really want to know." I assured her that I was willing to listen and reminded her of her salvation. She finally agreed and told me, "I'm being held captive!" Yes—I was stunned! I reached high to remain composed, and she waited for my reaction.

I asked her to share with me what she was able concerning the circumstances surrounding her captivity. She explained that she was an unwilling sexual object of lesbians and shielding her finger discretely pointed-out the house where she was being held under duress. She went on to tell me about the obsessiveness of the dwelling's other occupants. Less than a block away from their observation, she was allowed to sit. Time was running out, and she needed to return to the house. I asked, "Would it be of assistance if I talked with them?" She warned me not to try visiting because she had been on the receiving end of their anger.

It was a regular occurrence for me to see her temporarily released to the shackled seating arrangement on a bench. I greeted her, but she discretely waved me away from talking with her. Then, there was no sign of her for weeks. I prayed for her safety, and God comforted me that she was alive. Even though, I had not seen her. Then thankfully one day, she showed-up at my door.

The young woman requested my assistance to formulate an escape plan. I prayed with her to God for guidance and an escape plan for her to go to her desired destination. I made a request of her to send me a note if possible after she had escaped. I also assisted her with a time frame to complete the plan because I promised to confirm her well-being. Because I was persistent about checking on her status, she urged me to be careful warning me of certain danger prior to her return to the house of her captivity.

I prayed to God for patience because I was anxious concerning communicating with my new friend. Acknowledging God for His guidance, I waited beyond the time line of her escape plan. Then, I went to the door and asked to speak with my friend. I waited; while, one of the abusive captors reluctantly ascended the staircase and sarcastically yelled my friend's name. With the caustic comments from the

Victims

house's other occupants, it alerted me to adhere to all of the young victim's warnings. The captor descended the staircase to report that my friend was asleep. Then, the same captor insisted that I was never again to inquire for my friend—emphasizing that I was not welcome and threatening that I would regret any another visit.

During the same time, I had the humble desire to epitomize in writing the relationship between God (the Heavenly Father) and a person who sought that fellowship. The following poem came to mind.

Important Time
Have you ever sat in a field
near a stream or a sparkling body of water.
Sitting and speaking to the Father.

He's there from the start
as you pour out your heart
never missing a word—you say.

He says, "I love you.
You're Mine.
It's important to take this to pray."

Thankfully, God inspired those words. So, I understood that I am not able to alter anything that God has planned. But, God has made me able to assist with His plan. It was in His—God's hands. It wasn't until recently when I realized that the only means for the captive young woman's escape was on God's timetable.

A couple of days later, unconscionably, the captor who threatened me beat on the door of my home demanding me to disclose the whereabouts of the victim. I told the captor that I have not had any communication with the victim which the captor must have known. The captor replied, "What are you accusing me of doing; you can't prove anything?" Without responding to the raging captor's question, I suggested that the police ought to honor a missing person's request and volunteered to telephone the police. The enraged captor was cowled in disgrace and exited my home without so much as word.

I never again heard from the raging captor. However months later, I did receive a letter with no return address. The letter's content contained just three words. It read, "I made it." The last time that I had spoken with her, I did mention to her that I'd write her story, so others may gain an awareness of homosexuality's coercion. The scripture that came to mind follows: Matthew 10.16: *"Behold, I send you out as sheep in the midst of wolves. Therefore be wise as serpents and harmless as doves."*

Because of the immense peer pressure that subjects a homosexual victim to tolerate continued abuse, the victim often concludes that the circumstance is precarious. Deliverance is not always instant.

This young woman found herself in a position where so many of us have been looking for acceptance among peers. It was human nature for her to desire acceptance. The initial condition of her acceptance was not openly revealed. Then, she was the object of the homosexual's assaults without her consent. None of the house's assailants sympathized with her. She prayed for deliverance from her assailants, and God answered her prayer.

A homosexual victim suffers haunting homosexual abuse. Hopefully, the victim identifies that Jesus is Lord—the Savior. Hebrews 4.15: *For we do not have a High Priest who cannot sympathize with our weaknesses, but was in all* points *tempted as* we are, yet *without sin.*

In the garden of Eden, God gave freedom to Adam and Eve with a restriction. The tree of the knowledge of good and evil was the restriction. The despair distinction between freedom and openness instigated dissension.

Surrendering to unnatural curiosity (enticement) is a sin that requires forgiveness. 1 John 1.9: *If we confess* our *sins, He is faithful and just to forgive us* our *sins and to cleanse us from all unrighteousness.* Somehow through God's mercy, forgiving an abuser is equally as important as forgiving one's own self. The Bible records some of the abuse that Jesus endured in Psalm 129.3 and Isaiah 53.5 for a victim's identification and complete deliverance from abuse.

Comprehensively, seek God's advice concerning restoration of a victim's mental, physical and environmental well-being. Moreover, God's prayer for patience along with peace and protection is the priority. Proverbs 2.8-12 confirm His plan: *He guards the paths of justice, and preserves the way of His saints. Then you will understand righteousness, justice, equity* and *every good path. When wisdom enters your heart, and knowledge is pleasant to your soul, discretion will preserve you; understanding will keep you, to deliver you from evil, from the man who speaks perverse things.*

A reputable Christian helpline with an opposite sex counselor is a possible option for a victim to consider as well as a reputable Christian church. Because of

Victims

a victim's perverse conversations with a person of the same-sex, more often than not, it is best to believe to counsel with a person of the opposite sex. With God all things are possible, but the abuse from the past needs to be resolved to cleanse a victim's soul. Initially, a victim's tendency to physically embrace members of the same-sex needs to be at least curbed. And with this, a victim's church needs to be understanding that the victim is in recovery. *A time to embrace, and a time to refrain from embracing,* as Ecclesiastes 3.5 implores.

Remember, when a person is drawn away through their own lust, the person is enticed. Even though, God tries to deter victimization. Please take heed to the following word of caution. The media has the ability to startle a believer of God. A television production is attractive and pushes the limits of its viewers through extremely convincing, elaborate and expensive displays of grandeur. God is a able to guide you with discretion to set some media participation parameters.

The time may not be right, or the need may not be genuine. The enticement to do something different formidably appeals to a victim as the pursuit of happiness. New technology literally has the ability to make the devil look like an angel. For, he disguises himself as an angel of light. 2 Peter 2.18: *For when they speak great swelling* words *of emptiness, they allure through the lusts of the flesh, through lewdness, the ones who have actually escaped from those who live in error.*

Cautiously, a person does not allow one's own self to be deceived into an adverse situation. After being delivered from a homosexual lifestyle, a victim needs to dedicate some time to prayer and reading the Word of God. Mark 9:28-29: *And when He had come into the house, His disciples asked Him privately, "Why could we not cast it out?" So He said to them, "This kind can come out by nothing but prayer and fasting."* To manifest salvation, a person needs to immerse one's own self in God's presence especially if the person has cohabited with homosexuals. 2 Peter 2.9: Then *the Lord knows how to deliver the godly out of temptations and to reserve the unjust under punishment for the day of judgment.*

If something similar happened to you, the manifestation of your recovery was worth the physical and mental abuse that our Savior endured. God's plan was to afford a person the opportunity to be delivered from the power of darkness. You have been forgiven and healed; even if in all of the world, you were the only person that accepted deliverance. You received God's Word of deliverance in Ephesians 2.8-9: *For by grace you have been saved through faith, and that not of yourself;* it is *the gift of God. Not of works, lest anyone should boast.*

If you or someone you know is still in need of deliverance, please consider attending a local church. Also, by typing key words "Free Online Christian Counseling" in an Internet search engine, a person is able to discover that some counseling is initially available with no fee or a minimum fee.

When you do make time to pray, find a area in your living space with little or no distractions. Please consider praying the following prayer: Heavenly Father: I've been in a bad situation. Strengthen me in your presence. Guide me on the road to recovery. Allow me the peace to remain on track with Your Word, in the name of the Lord and Savior Jesus, Amen. Additionally, it's comforting to meditate on Isaiah 49.16: *See, I have inscribed you on the palms* of My hands. Because you love God, meditate on His Word of deliverance, and let not the world distract you from Jesus' deliverance. As always if you are in need of medical assistance, please seek assistance. God is able to work with you under the medical care of the proper physician.

Be not fearful of the raging politically correct tides. Constitutional self-evidence needs no verification. "You can't prove that" is the frequent plea of the guilty. As a defensive stance, a homosexual lobbying group continues to propound for preferential rights and not equal rights to instigate homosexuality's agenda.

For "Constitutionally Correct" thinking people, provident decisions guard unalienable rights for the next generation and are axiomatic. God respecting people accept the grace and peace to see invisible things; while, unbelievers refuse as revealed in Romans 1.20 and follows. *For since the creation of the world His invisible* attributes *are clearly seen, being understood by the things that are made,* even *His eternal power and Godhead, so that they are without excuse.* Not all people accept their ability to see the inevitable. Today's so-called "progressive" changes more often than not are expensive, experimental and deceptive because traditional wisdom is challenged. Self-evidence's propositions are axiomatic and are not exceptions to the people's common welfare. Unconstitutionally, homosexuality's detriments oppose traditional wisdom, natural order and the administration thereof.

Chapter 3
The Origin Indicates the Outcome

A homosexual who is oblivious to abuse has difficulty accepting that unnatural affection isn't on the the "top ten list" of things to do in the Bible. Once in awhile, I hear that someone says, "Jesus never talks about homosexuality." That's simply because "homosexuality" is a fairly recent term.

Jesus didn't dwell on the particular details of sin. He identified sin, so a soul repented. Jesus' "fire and brimstone" teaching made six direct references to the consequences of Sodom and Gomorrah's sin.

Ministers, priests and rabbis realized that too many wrath-filled teachings haven't encouraged attendance on Sunday. Teachings with more emphasis on grace, mercy and peace encouraged attendance. Teachings on the wrath still have a place in a person's heart. After all, God and the Lord Jesus delivered us from the wrath to come.

A homosexual victim that is enlightened to abuse still seeks closure. Even though homosexuality is formidably abandoned as psychiatric medical condition, homosexual abuse always has been a political issue in America. Resolving unnatural homosexual abuse remains a right protected under the Laws of Nature and Nature's God in the *Declaration of Independence*.

Instead of the American Psychiatric Association (APA) adhering to its ethical and foundational medical practice, the APA's Committee on Nomenclature agreed to delete "homosexuality" replacing it with "sexual orientation disturbance." Historically in 1970, the APA Conference was invaded in San Francisco, California with the protesting of homosexuals. Peaceful assembly outside was permissible, but the protest somehow was made an APA Conference issue of contention. The same occurred in 1971 at the APA Conference located in Washington, D.C. Because homosexuality was included in the compendium of psychiatric disorders of the APA, the revolt of the homosexual protesters demanded that the psychiatric history of the homosexual abuse was prejudiced. For homosexuals whom abandon self-evidence, justice was viewed as vindicative.

The homosexual protest continued in its annoyance at the APA's Annual Conferences. Then, the APA's Board of Trustees deleted homosexuality from the the list of mental illnesses in the APA's diagnostic manual in late 1973 and instituted the omission in early 1974. Members of the board attempted to overturn the 1974 decision during the same year without success. Since then, the board has been approached to reverse its coerced decision without consequence. The absence of the diagnosis of homosexual abuse has not been congruent with the Constitution, but homosexual lobbying has capitalized on the omission of the medical confirmation for victims of homosexuality. The board succumbed to intimidation because of the homosexuals' disturbing verbal annoyance.

Because the APA has refused to publicly report homosexuality's detriments, victims of homosexuality self-evidently are offered a prescription instead of behavioral therapy to restore victims from the abuse. According to the *Archives of General Psychiatry's* http://archpsyc.ama-assn.org/ website, the number of people using antidepressant prescriptions have increased from 13.3 to 27.0 million persons between 1995 and 2005. Antidepressant prescriptions have more than doubled over a 10 year period.

Variations of historical perspectives may confirm or contradict the preceding self-evident account. To my knowledge, no other diseases have been wiped-out with an eraser in the history of humankind. Diseases like homosexuality are harmful when untreated. Quite possibly, some general practitioners still treat or refer some victims of homosexual abuse. Consequently, the physical and psychological ramifications of homosexual abuse are now not required to report for public consideration. The detriments of the APA's dismissal of homosexuality adopt a covert stance of tolerance and self-evidently confirms extreme methods of instigation. Consequentially with volatile names on the door, homosexuals are not out of the closet.

Complacency, concerning a homosexual abuse victim's inability to confirm abuse hinders the American culture. It's common knowledge that a homosexual abuse victim is less likely to report abuse because of the prolonged humiliation of the abuse. Categorizing all homosexuals in one group is ignorant. Clearly, homosexuality thrives on the deception that there is no abuser; while, somewhere a homosexual abuse victim continues to be abused.

What's sexually right is misappropriated in our society as individually objective. Acceptance of the common welfare of the people isn't the foundation for proposed homosexual legislation. For example, so-called "civil rights" lobbyists continue to influence sexual education legislation. For sexual assailants, the right thing is the normalization of emotional, financial and physical harm for their pursuit of happiness.

It's not immediately apparent, but a same-sex union interferes with human rights. An ulterior motive is apparent when posing the question, "Does homosexuality stand for preserving traditional marriage in addition to instituting a same-sex relationship?" Traditional marriage under the Laws of Nature and Nature's God is superfluous to advocates of same-sex union legislation. If a same-sex union redefines traditional marriage under the unnatural standard of a same-sex union, an unnatural law then defines the acceptance of human extinction.

I served as an elected student representative in student government during my years in compulsory as well as post-secondary education. At every level, the issue of homosexual rights was proposed as an issue. As a student representative, a question that I verbalized was, "Doesn't a homosexual already have human rights under the Constitution just like everyone else?"

As an example, I was rushing to my next class, and a teacher flagged me down. He gasped and said, "Do you have a moment?" I nodded in agreement; even though, it wasn't the most convenient time. He continued, "I'd like you to propose a charter for a new club for the students. Because it's a new club, the charter needs to be requested by a student." I said, "Okay." With some anxiety, he specified the following: "Not so quick; the request is to charter a Student Gay and Lesbian Club." Not at all foreign to me, I requested clarification, "Alright, they're going to ask what the homosexual club's objectives are, so what are they?'"

Looking perplexed, the homosexual club's advocate delivered an unusually long pregnant-pause expecting me to supply the answer. Uncertain, I suggested that the homosexual club's purpose was possibly to have "equal rights and freedom from prejudice." With increasing anxiety, he corrected me, "It's not a homosexual club; it's a Student Gay and Lesbian Club—are you prejudice?" I replied, "No—no, I'm just requesting the information in order to present the proposal of the club's charter. Is there a student that you know who is willing to come forward to verify the request, and are you willing to be the club's supervisor? Also, does your sponsoring organization have a web address because the administrative board may request verification of a sponsor's credibility?" With another pregnant-pause, he grimaced, wrote the sponsor's website on a piece of scrap paper and concluded, "I want to be anonymous. I don't care what you do—just get the club's charter."

Well, what initially appeared as an innocuous request turned into duress. Lack of accountability led me to think that he was hiding something. Not without foundation, because, he didn't supply a single objective for the organization. Because I was exploited, I didn't feel obligated to make the request to the student government's administrative board.

I wrestled with God whether or not to propose the homosexual club's charter because I did not want to be subjected to duress. So, I acknowledged God and did some initial research on this particular sponsor's website. The website didn't provide any substantial information to merit the homosexual club's charter or contribute for the presentation to the board.

At the next board meeting, I presented the Student Gay and Lesbian Club's charter with the information that I suggested to the club's anonymous adviser. The administrative board anticipated all of the questions that I proposed. The anonymity of the advocate was accepted without question. During the discussion, I recommended the verification of the sponsor's credibility as an opposing point of reference because the sponsor's website supplied no apparent attribute for its organization. However, the board still accepted the homosexual club's charter proposal for consideration.

The club's anonymous advocate checked with me on a regular basis. For months, he inquired and retreated with the request. My response appeared inconsequential with his back to me, and the distance between us increased beyond the normal range of hearing. I continued to follow through with my responsibility with inquiries concerning the board's decision on the club's charter. After three months of requests, a representative of the administrative board responded with some ambivalence, "Oh, that was done a long time ago!"

Upon reflection, I believed that God wanted me to oppose the charter to expose the deception. The advocate didn't know a single semi-legitimate objective for the club and was embarrassed for his inability to provide an objective. The substantiation that I requested from the advocate was repeated back to me by the administrative board like a script. Substantiation of the club's credibility to institute the club's charter was obtrusive. When I reported the installation of the club's charter to the advocate, he looked smugly at me without saying a word and walked away.

At the following meeting, the administrative board expected me to respond concerning the homosexual club's response to the board's decision. I didn't consider it my obligation to cover-up the the indignant response from the homosexual club's adviser. Nor, did I. I simply said, "I thought the club was pleased." The board didn't appear pleased with my response. The board probed me for additional gratitude, but the indignation of the homosexual club's adviser instigated no appreciation to communicate.

I was thoroughly disappointed that the board didn't require substantiation of credibility and approved the homosexual club. The advocate for the homosexual club (unfruitful works of darkness) determined no need for justification or reciprocation. God assisted me to voice initial opposition because of the club's absence of credibility as Ephesians 5.11-12 reveals: *Have no fellowship with the unfruitful works of darkness, but rather expose* them. *For it is shameful even to speak of those things which are done by them in secret.* The lascivious act of homosexuality was never elaborated in the Bible and was not expected to be mentioned by believers.

For the purpose of this writing, support, youth and other designated groups are comprehensively identified as "homosexual clubs." Homosexual clubs go by a variety of elusive names and acronyms. The "Unfruitful Works of Darkness" and "Abusers of Themselves With Humankind" aren't the comprehensive identities that homosexual clubs adopt. Instead, "Safe Schools" and "Safe Sex" with a homosexual philosophy at the center are evident departures from public education's ability to comprehensively label.

Initially, sexual education was expanded through legislation with the promise of reducing teenage pregnancy and sexually transmitted diseases (STDs). The opposite resulted with the irresponsible sexual education discussed too early in primary education for decades. The average age of consensual sex was established to protect children 16 years-of-age and younger in the majority of states. Unplanned pregnancies, STDs and sexual abuse escalated. Responsible sexual education recommended some abstinence instruction, but abstinence has been misinterpreted as religious.

So-called "homosexual rights" activists are condoning the cycle of sexual abuse through proposing legislation to add the words "or sexual orientation" to the *US Constitution*. Sexual orientation's definitions are nefarious because of sexual predators' and rapists' esoteric interpretations. Race, color, creed and national origin are inherent human characteristics. Historically, the majority of homosexuals still admit that they were victims of childhood sexual abuse.

The following premise has been erroneously tolerated, "What's has gone on in their bedroom hasn't hurt anyone else." Therefore, this logic has been flawed in the acknowledgment that their actions have been hurtful to themselves. This prevarication has been further propounded because homosexual lobbying has continued to be tolerated with the US Department of Education and the teachers' union. Under the guise of equal rights, homosexual lobbying has expanded homosexual views beyond the bedroom and has hampered sexual perspectives for children. With unconstitutional justification, sexual orientation has been aggressively pursued in primary education without scrutiny."

My quest to expose homosexual clubs' deception continued when I discovered that homosexual clubs were instituted in primary education. I challenged the premature exposure of adult sexual subjects for children. Through numerous letters that addressed education's administrators, I questioned, "Why has public education allowed the presence of a homosexual clubs in primary education?" The consensus that I received in response from my letters was that homosexual support groups addressed problems which confronted children. Even though, the age of consensual sex was clearly communicated in my letters which expressed concern that children have been prematurely exposed to adult sexual issues. Because public education has instituted homosexual clubs, homosexuality's philosophy has attempted to exonerate unnatural behavior. Although children have been too young for sexual activity, institution of homosexual clubs' philosophy has tolerated that unnatural homosexual behavior was "all good."

The intent of the *Constitution of the United States* is expounded in the first paragraph of the *Declaration of Independence*. "The separate and equal station to which the Laws of Nature and Nature's God entitle them." Mercilessly, sexual education's curricula chooses to sacrifice the sexual perception of children, so some adult's sexual orientation isn't insulted.

Sexual knowledge that was introduced in close proximity to the legal age of consensual sex would have been proactive. Prematurely mandating sexual education to children too many years before legal activity has been oppressive. Enforced in 2002 with the "No Child Left Behind Act of 2001," "equal access" was instituted for youth groups regardless of sexual orientation as an concession (earmark). A combined keyword search revealed the same with "No Child Left Behind Act of 2001"+"sexual orientation" on http://www.gpo.gov and http://find.ed.gov websites. As a result, the Department of Education's mission was: "To ensure equal access to education and to promote educational excellence throughout the nation." Presently, its mission has evolved: "To promote student achievement and preparation for global competitiveness by fostering educational excellence and ensuring equal access."

When homosexuality's behaviors are no longer limited to scopes of their own bedrooms, children below the age of consensual sex are influenced. Because homosexuals have sought "equal access" through legislation, homosexuals have sought premature and illiberal acceptance from children. Therefore, homosexuals have crossed the line and exposed the need to appeal legislation.

Consequently, some justified affirmations follow:

- A homosexual doesn't just want to be left alone.
- Homosexuality hurts someone else.
- Eliminating the scope of homosexuality's influence is a priority.
- Rescinding campus privileges to an employee's same-sex partner.
- Curbing sexual orientation's provocative speech.
- Eliminating distribution of sexually orientated materials to children.
- A same-sex couple's union is not equal to traditional marriage.
- Equal access for any sexual orientation group is counterproductive.

When gender identification and sexual orientation are incorrectly assessed as educational issues, children below the age of consensual sex are exposed to adult sexual subjects. Most of public education's administration, faculty and in-house homosexual clubs have extreme difficulty distinguishing between pedagogy and andragogy because of homosexuals' peer pressure (codependency to curricula coercion).

If public education and the homosexual clubs had honored the age of consensual sex, they may have maintained some respect from adults through humane adherence to consensual sex laws. Moreover, sexual inhibitions of children ought to have been respected as natural development because they are not emotionally, financially or physically equipped to sustain adult sexual relationships. Many pubic educators have scoffed at "the innocence of children" because with sexual education children have been denied their innocence.

What is being compromised? The public is mourning the loss of philosophical input concerning education for children. Public education proclaims in its mantra, "We know what's best for the children." It's not a minor issue. It's big. Public sexual education's amorphous curricula including illiberal politics is based on illegitimate homosexual liberty addressing children regardless of age. When moral conversation suggests a traditional approach, the conversation is declared religious. A proven track record is dismissed, so public education is empowered with the unconstitutional latitude to institute open access (an illiberal track). Then, Constitutionally moral conversation is ignored. The perversion of the "Let's agree to disagree" philosophy too often results in untimely legislation that dismisses parents' provident opinions. The philosophy's origin hasn't hailed from the halls of public education, but sexual education's lobbying redefines the philosophy to suit its oppressive agenda.

According to Wikopedia's http://en.wikipedia.org/wiki/John_Wesley website, John Wesley has been attributed with coining the current version of the phrase: "Let's agree to disagree." John Wesley spoke of agreeing to disagree with George Whitefield. A spirited discussion concerning personal opinions on predestination did not preclude their association? Therefore, harmony was mutually agreed upon to function within the Methodist Church.

John Wesley rolled over in his grave when public education opposed anything moral and misinterpreted his philosophy. Case and point, public education's so-called "transparent" sexual education did not practice well-informed communication but eluded from full disclosure. In other words, sexual education declared itself "infallible" and rejected provident input. So, public education fully implemented an immoral sexual education curricula without sufficient scrutiny.

Public education apparently describes the behavior of people who vocalize their discontent with the uncivil sexual education program as "uncivil." To be true to transparency if a local school board doesn't want to consider public input, then, don't ask for it. Eye-rolling indicates public education's attitude of presenting a deaf ear to the citizens' suggestions.

Math and English are justified, fundamental subjects that the US Department of Education ought to be capable of instituting—agreed? But, volatile adult issues like gender identification and sexual orientation are arbitrary and not to be dictated through curricula. The US Department of Education and local school boards need to exhibit fortitude and correctly analyze that adult homosexuals have no business influencing sexual orientation for children.

On June 5, 2008, the Minnesota Department of Health's http://www.health.state.mn.us website listed its five-year plan to prevent sexual violence that included: "Seeking action by public and private policy entities." The Message Action Team's goal for its Suggested Six-Month Work Plan dated September 15, 2009 listed:

Strengthen social norms that encourage healthy and respectful relationships. One of the implementation strategies listed: "Evaluate existing social marketing campaigns and develop new ones where appropriate, to support healthy relationships and counter the normalization of sexual harm."

Andragogy in primary education instead of pedagogy has redefined sexuality as, "It's all good." Appropriately in 2004, the Minnesota State Legislature's http://www.house.leg.state.mn.us/hrd/bs/83/HF0580.html website presented abstinence in a program titled "Comprehensive Sexual Education." Because the CSE bill's progress considered real comprehensive sexual issues, the bill halted. Impeded because—abstinence was presented in support of a healthy and natural relationship. Now, public education's own definition of a CSE Program has been endorsed by homosexual clubs.

A homosexual club uses its own definition of CSE and does not benefit from real comprehensive sexual education. Same-sex marriage's untimely legislation attributing some financial responsibility to an unnatural relationship has denied homosexuality's emotional and physical detriments. Any attempt that a homosexual club has portrayed to personify a homosexual relationship with marginal responsibility has been superficial and does not respect the institution of traditional marriage. Because of a homosexual club's disregard for traditional or Constitutional marriage, it's a miracle that a child emerges from public education with moral bearings and is a testament to the power of God's Word.

Public education now accepts antisocial behavior as normal. It's imperative that education's paradigm reverses its acceptance of unconstitutional behavior. Because public education doesn't currently support moral education, public education's curricula content condones unnatural behavior denying origins and outcomes. It's time to reexamine the origins of sexual orientation. But, it's axiomatic that sexual abuse remains the major contributing factor for a victim to choose homosexuality.

In the true sense of the word "progress," it ought to mean that appropriate education decreases premature sexual activity along with the associated physical maladies. Instead of decreasing the teenage pregnancy percentage, teenage pregnancy is increasing. So, a comprehensive initiative to reduce teenage pregnancy has been substituted with the idea that teenagers can have sex with birth control education. The conundrum has culminated with the unspoken realization, "Why would children responsibly implement birth control during sex when casual sexual education instructors reduce children to sexual objects?"

Proportionate abstinence in sexual education instruction to children promotes emotional, financial and physical responsibility. The inappropriate usage of the word "safe" in contraception has resulted in the escalation of unplanned teenage pregnancies. Has public education become more civilized or less civilized? Allowing prepubescent children to be incomprehensibly instructed in sexual education hasn't been timely.

Inadvertently, many parents are denying sexual education's role in the premature sexual activity of children. Consequently, they assess no potential harm for the continuation of an ineffective sexual education curriculum.

Instead of advocacy for reporting inappropriate sexual advances, public education's counseling reports on sexual abuse are declining. Public education's counselors confront homosexual victims who are seeking comfort with the following question: "Are you having difficulty accepting your sexuality?" When allegations are brought to authorities, character witnesses from the same institution of learning contradict the veracity of victims. Without the corroboration verifying victims' assaults, education's faculty and staff members contribute to the normalization of sexual harm.

Numerous social and economic challenges are eminent because of underestimating the consequences of ineffective sexual education. The US Social Services Department is evidencing the emotional, financial and physical ramifications of irresponsibly educated children. Nevertheless, the US Department of Education continues to support its premature implementation of its sexual education program.

Although, traditional marriage is not perfect. With provident consideration, public education has the ability to favorably view traditional families and make a beneficial contribution to reverse vital statistics' immoral trends. The marriage relationship communicates life-long intentions. There's refuge in traditional marriage. It's a wife's responsibility and privilege to contribute in common goals with her husband. Likewise, it's a husband's natural responsibility and privilege to participate emotionally, financially and physically. 1 Corinthians 7.4 reads: *The wife does not have authority over her own body, but the husband* does. *And likewise the husband does not have authority over his own body, but the wife* does.

Determining the difference between what is genuine or what is deception requires God's assistance. Paul, the apostle, attempts to convince the people of Corinth that he acknowledged God in his communication in 1 Corinthians 2.4: *And my speech and my preaching* were *not with persuasive words of human wisdom, but in*

Victims

demonstration of the Spirit and of power. God warns us about an unbeliever's enticing words. Colossians 2.4 records the following: *Now this I say lest anyone should deceive you with persuasive words.*

Additionally, the inhabitants of Babel thought that contradicting God would usurp their destiny in Genesis 11.3-4: *Then they said to one another, "Come, let us make bricks and bake them thoroughly." They had brick for stone, and they had asphalt for mortar. And they said, "Come, let us build ourselves a city, and a tower whose top* is *in the heavens; let us make a name for ourselves, lest we be scattered abroad over the face of the whole earth."* The inhabitants didn't acknowledge God, so their own construction plans resulted in the inability to communicate with each other, their dispersion on the earth and a city named "Babel."

A collaborative project needs God's guidance. For instance with this writing, I acknowledge God in order to present godly and decisive information including praying for you as a reader. My belief is that God inspires and strengthens you in your everyday life and future aspirations. Relying on God's guidance enriches the lives of the people to honestly recognize progress.

The Founding Fathers esteemed the relevance of acknowledging the Creator and follows, "And for the support of this Declaration, with a firm reliance on the protection of divine Providence, we mutually pledge our Lives, our Fortunes and our sacred Honor."

PART 2
THE CREATOR'S MEANING OF LIBERTY IN THE US CONSTITUTION

Precious words from a child's perspective: "We're free in the U' States 'cause the Cr'ater gave us Liberty. And, it's not 'structive (destructive) 'cause Liberty is the second, big gift."

Chapter 4
The Outcome Indicates the Origin

To occupy my grandson in the car, I handed him my pocket New Testament, courtesy of the Gideons. My granddaughter enjoyed leafing through the pages and asking Bible questions when we traveled. It seemed like a good idea to continue the tradition because my granddaughter identified with the child-size treasure.

I heard a ripping sound and resigned myself to the fact that a page may need mending. I inquisitively asked my grandson, "What was that?" Without a response, I kept my eyes on the road. It was dark and cold when we arrived at our destination. I unbuckled him from his car seat and sheltered him from the weather as we escaped from the elements.

With a busy schedule, it was a number of days before I discovered the Bible without its cover. Searching the backseat, I found that the cover had been separated from the binding and placed both in my lapel pocket to later repair. I related the incident to my wife, and she responded with a chuckle commenting that my grandson is in need of some instruction and strong, too.

When the pastor referenced a scripture the following Sunday, I retrieved my Bible to view the scripture. At the end of the sermon, I shifted the detached cover and the seams just didn't appear to match up. Then, I opened the Bible and looked at the cover and realized that the cover was upside down.

Once the damage was properly assessed, I realized that the repair would be easy with a little glue. Thankfully, I hadn't glued the cover on upside down. Even though, the damage was a little more serious. The assessment now was clear to proceed in the right direction to make the repair.

I didn't explain that the pocket Bible was not a toy to my grandson as I had with my granddaughter. When the Bible initially ripped, I underestimated the damage. Later, I overestimated the repair because the pieces didn't appear to come together. It wasn't until I opened the Bible and aligned it with the cover that the assessment was properly estimated nearly a week later.

It's not a disgrace to initially underestimate a problem. However when a problem is more serious, an assessment needs compensation to resolve a situation. Nor is it a disgrace to initially overestimate a challenge. But when all of the facts are assessed, the solution is resolved accordingly. Not making time to properly assess a problem may result in disgrace especially when neglect or complacency compounds the problem.

With an honest assessment, making time with my grandson to properly instruct him is the solution. It is important for my grandson to understand the difference between a toy and a book that ought to be respected. After all, it's the grace from the Bible that has literally saved my life.

Natural characteristics that we have in common unit us and not exceptions to the norm. During our lives, we all have a biological mother and a father. Thankfully, the *Declaration of Independence* and the *Constitution of the United States* recognize that the things most important to all of us are what we have in common.

Diversity in itself does not make our Nation great. It's the variety of people uniting under one banner of freedom that makes the people in the US great.

The Declaration of Independence and the *US Constitution* recognize the marriage relationship with many statements including "secure the blessings of liberty to ourselves and our posterity." We remember to exercise our freedom of speech and respond with a proactive alternative against threats when traditional marriage's sanctity is threatened.

People of all cultures are not ignorant that a variety of human relationships are important, but without the unions between men and women, none of those bonds are even possible. Relationships between men and women are foundational to our Nation's infrastructure. Proverbs 30.18-19 (KJV) reads: *There be three* things which *are too wonderful for me, yea, four which I know not. The way of an eagle in the air, the way of a serpent upon a rock, the way of a ship in the midst of the sea, and the way of a man with a maid.*

We are all so unique with different challenges. We know that some same-sex relationships have children from a natural relationship. Inherently, same-sex unions don't carry equal responsibility, so Constitutional marriages are exclusive for men with women.

We determine that vital things are for the common good like "we hold these truths to be self-evident that all men are created equal." Since incompatibility occurs between lesbians and gay men, same-sex relationships' inherent traits ultimately threaten the human race's existence. Homosexuals usurp disdain and misdirect the absence of a dignified response with assaults on the natural development of children through premature sexual education. In other words, criticisms of the sexual clubs' presence in public education ought to be outrageous. We surrender in silence under the guise of prejudice when we're stunned and confused.

Have the general population's passions been misconstrued? Two factors, origins and outcomes are misrepresented or ignored. Respectively, "Oh-oh!" or "Oh!" responses vary in their perception but distinctly define self-serving or serving the common good. Origins and outcomes are indicative of the nature of an issue. For example, the outcomes of the overwhelming practical application of same-sex unions ultimately are volatility and extinction. The origins of same-sex unions more often than not aren't scrutinized.

Prejudices revolve around ignorance. Constitutional liberties that are documented such as the Constitution and this writing are not meant to harm homosexuals and don't. Like the majority of Americans, homosexuals are horrified when an act of violence appears to directly assault the group's sexual orientation.

The perpetrator of any murder violates the law and is subject to punishment in accordance with the crime. The so-called "Hate Crimes Act" erroneously instigates legislation that supersedes violent crimes laws and misappropriates subcultures of people. In the final draft, the bill attempts to include people of different sexual orientations, disabilities and races.

The motives for murder are all unjustifiable and have ignorance and jealousy as catalysts. Deaths occurring through self defense are legally justifiable. All murders are a threat on the human race, and all subcultures belong to one or more cultures of the human race. *The US Constitution's* rights outline protection from acts of violence against the human race. Race, color, creed and national origin encompass all cultures of the human race.

Though all murders in America have not been without mourning, homosexual murder victims like all murder victims previously belonged to crimes against the human race. The mourners have been victimized, too. Victimized in that, their losses are life-long. In cases when homosexuals have been the mortality statistics, mourners have proven not to be satisfied with justice that the assailants receive; even though, the sentences have been consistent in the prosecution of other murder crimes.

President Barack Obama signed the Hate Crimes Act on October 28, 2009. As a division of the National Defense Authorization Act for 2010 (H.R. 2647). The Matthew Shepard and James Byrd Jr. Hate Crimes Prevention Act, was instigated for a homosexual victim and an African-American victim, respectively. The lobbying capitulated the mourners' states of closure and sensationalized subcultural murders. Previous to the legislation, each of these murders like other arraigned crimes of murder arrived at a verdict. Constitutionally, the legal system still prosecuted the guilty and sentenced the perpetrators.

Even though the Hate Crimes Act contributes little if any comfort to mourners, it does initially satisfy homosexuality's agenda. Honestly, homosexuality's political agenda does not contribute benefits to the common welfare of the American people. Like other homosexual legislation, the Hate Crimes Act evades the horrendous detriments that are inherent with the homosexual subculture through partnering with a legitimate cultural right.

Indiana Representative Mike Pence articulated, "Hate crimes provisions in this legislation, as before, are antithetical to those First Amendment traditions and unnecessary."

An excerpt from Alexander Hamilton's introductory letter in support of the *Declaration of Independence* and the *US Constitution* to National newspapers and published in the *Federalist Papers* reads: "It will be forgotten, on the one hand, that jealousy is the usual concomitant of violent love, and that the noble enthusiasm of liberty is too apt to be infected with a spirit of narrow and illiberal distrust." Alexander Hamilton's reference to "illiberal" exposes the unconstitutional objectives of special interest groups that are not for the common good.

The Declaration of Independence was interpreted as treasonous from the Great Britain's aristocratic perspective. However, the *Declaration of Independence* with the *Constitution of the United States, The Bill of Rights and The Emancipation Proclamation* had been described collectively as the greatest "Documents of Freedom."

Constitutionally, homosexuals already have protection against illegal acts of violence. Both, Mike Pence and Alexander Hamilton's words exhibit the rarely exemplified political characteristic of timeless wisdom. Whereas, same-sex relationships' pursuits for preferential rights and not equal rights are short-sighted.

When the Constitution's freedoms are no longer appreciated, liberties are redefined without provident consideration. Narrow and illiberal opinions are propagated with prevarication. Since same-sex unions' propensities already have inhibited procreation, homosexual relationships haven't been provident.

At one time, the word "wise" was used to describe our Nation's political leaders. One such saying exemplified providence and follows, "Ask not what your Country can do for you—ask what you can do for your Country." In contrast to providence, homosexuality's philosophy has now been instituted in public education under the guise of freedom.

Same-sex relationships also want legal declaration that they may marry; even though, homosexual unions haven't been a political institution practically since the beginning of time.

Some people may conclude that Mike Pence and Alexander Hamilton are "homophobic." Others may conclude that homosexuals' jealousies are fueling narrow and illiberal distrust in the Constitution.

Unlike the Constitution, the Hate Crimes Act is a waste of space on the hard drives that it occupies. The fact remains that same-sex relationships are not provident including contemptible ramifications pawned-off on the next generation—our posterity.

A same-sex relationship implies that a man doesn't need a woman, and a woman doesn't require a man to sustain the human race. The sexual objectivity that was renounced with the Women's Rights movement is being forfeited with the pursuit of homosexual rights.

Why is public education's sexual education ignoring the following facts while exposing children below the age of consensual sex to adult sexual subjects?

- Overwhelming acceptance of domestic partnerships, civil unions and same-sex marriage propagates extinction.

- Same-sex relationships imply that a man doesn't need a woman, and a woman doesn't require a man to sustain the human race.
- It's illegal for children below the age of consensual to engage in sexual activity, so for an adult teacher to prematurely instruct sexual practices implies conspiracy tolerating statutory rape.
- Children are not emotionally, financially or physically mature enough to responsibly bear the burden of sexual relationships.
- Why would children responsibly implement birth control during sex when casual sexual education instructors reduce children to sexual objects?
- The residence of homosexual clubs (support groups) in primary education isn't perceived as encouraging premature sexual behavior with children below the age of consensual sex.
- With subtlety, the age of consensual sex is challenged in compulsory education with children exposed to homosexual clubs under the guise of equal rights; while, supporting traditional marriage is minimally addressed.

In consideration of these facts, it is impossible for a domestic partnership, civil union or same-sex marriage to equal traditional marriage's responsibility. Homosexual marriage's proponents quite often include traditional marriage in legislation; while, traditional marriage is already legal. Reciprocal ploys are evidence of homosexuality's convoluted legislation and are meant to be dissected and refuted.

An institution like public education initially appears to be a wise choice to educate our young people. But, instituting so-called "progressive" knowledge isn't provident. Public education's obtrusive curricula dictates the following philosophy, "Public education is not a democratic institution." This dictatorial education institution results in an inadequately educated generation that needs to be re-educated in the rudiments of life. So in this case, pubic education isn't part of the solution because casual sexual education dictates that parents and children surrender to its ideology.

Deviation from traditional definitions of terminology has arrived at the juncture of public education describing injustice as "justice" and supporting the same. Without an adherence to a standard of truth, the spoken word has been misinterpreted. Pubic education has instigated a prejudicial connotation to sexually questioning, "What's right or wrong?" Education hasn't been the answer.

Victims

Comprehensive education may be the answer. Traditionally defined comprehensive education is the answer as long as comprehensive isn't limited under a homosexually biased scope in meaning.

Is all homosexuality sexual abuse? Literally, physically and politically—yes! Homosexuality is sexual abuse. Literally, improper use is abuse. Physically, proper use would not harm the body. Politically, transient sexual abuse is unnatural.

Confused perspectives concerning homosexuals' sexuality and human identity have perpetuated sexual abuse. All victims of homosexual orientation have been abused. Victims are confused and in denial. Abused victims have wanted other people to accept homosexuality's identity and deny the abuse. Instead of homosexuals respecting their human nature and humanity, homosexuals have preferred that their perversions define who they are. Homosexuality's evasive detriments overwhelmingly expose homosexuality's denial to honor human existence.

Legislative assaults to lower the age of consensual sex are the obtrusive issues that bypass well-informed consideration. When children are being homosexually abused, homosexuals' opinions pervade concerning victims' acceptance and normalization of homosexual abuse. Honestly, young students are quite often unable to receive Constitutionally natural advice from school counselors. More often than not, school counselors erroneously accept homosexuality as humanitarian. When abused children need comfort and restoration of their dignity, school counselors are confronting victims with the acceptance of their homosexuality. Without comfort, counselors suggest that children are seducing their assailants. Then, children feel the humiliation and shame from homosexual abuse because school counselors deny homosexual abuse.

Acceptance of homosexual abuse as normal sexual activity is a perversion. How is it possible for a biased homosexual to resolve a homosexually abused child's issues when the homosexual has unresolved issues? Who's to help these victims of homosexual abuse? Certainly, the public education system isn't expressing interest in helping children deal with homosexual abusers. Its interests reside in reinforcing young people with the acceptance of homosexuality.

A word of caution, please be vigilant concerning "Safe Room" inquiries at your local school. What confronts you is so-called "confidentiality" often accompanied with sincere denial or total deception. Like removing a quill from a porcupine, your inquiry evokes the illiberal response similar to the following, "Homosexuality isn't hurting anyone." Homosexual abuse hurts people.

Also, a term like "alternative" is misleading. Sexual education exposes children to the concept that something as destructive as homosexual abuse is an alternative. For example, a homosexual support group or homosexual club substitutes the word "disgrace" for the misnomer "pride." Sexual education's standard accepts homosexuality's paradox of confusion in daily education for children. Public education struggles with the question, "Who's to say, what is right or wrong?" Here's something enlightening for educators. Abuse is always wrong. Homosexuality is abuse. Regretfully, teaching a sexual education curricula that condones homosexuality borders on a statutory rape conspiracy.

No doubt, homosexuals need help. And, not all victims surrender to the abuse in which they are victims. Victims seeking restoration or recovery through practical or Christian counseling are able to regain confidence with sound counseling. Psalms 107.20: *He (God) sent His word and healed them, and delivered* them *from their destructions.* School administrators and teachers are among the first who need to regain a proper perspective. Counseling and education that adhere to Constitutional concepts are better alternatives than condoning sexual abuse.

Legalization of a domestic partnership, homosexual union or same-sex marriage is a blatant contradiction of the *Declaration of Independence*. Politically, ordaining a same-sex relationship instigates a volatile institution and lacks providence.

We may find that it's difficult to imagine any unnatural events occurring in the Eighteenth Century. Yet, the *Declaration of Independence* proclaims, "The separate and equal station to which the Laws of Nature and Nature's God entitle them." Were the British polluting the Potomac? Semantically, when we hear of unnatural events, we envision oil spills and dead creatures washed-up on beaches. But, detriments of aristocracies that mandate unnatural subservience are exposed in the Constitution. In other words, laws that allow the ruling class to unnaturally exploit its nation's citizens are barbarous. If instituting homosexual relationship's ordinances aren't considered a transient political issue, may we assume that the people will be enlightened when no children are being born?

Can violating the Laws of Nature and Nature's God result in a national disaster? We need to consider one of the worst possible scenarios: The majority of the people agree that same-sex marriage should be an American institution (legalized). No children are being born. Under government order, lesbians are forced to procreate with gays or be artificially inseminated to prolong the human race. Then because of the lack compatibility and chemistry, infertility and volatility pervade.

Victims

Real freedom doesn't violate the rights of others. As the saying goes, "It's not good to fool mother nature." Because of public sexual education's dictation of homosexuality's perception for children, is it too late to ensure that the next generation does not endorse the national institution of same-sex marriage?

Damage control isn't a strong suit of national disaster relief organizations. Public policy's misunderstanding of the Constitution including the separation between church and state currently affects all of us in America. In addition, public education underestimates the value of faith-based organizations' physical presence during a disaster with prayer, food and clothing. While, a national disaster relief organization like the Federal Emergency Management Agency (FEMA) stalls through paperwork.

The truth concerning the separation of church and state is that no single religion should be the only endorsed religion by our Government, and any unauthorized religion is therefore alienated. It's imperative to maintain a policy of cooperation with faith-based organizations. So if an injured disaster victim requests prayer for God's help, the same victim has access to take a sip of water if the Government supplies a bottle of water. This example may appear like common sense. However, a certain civil rights lobbying organization currently opposes faith-based organizations' prayer in disaster relief. Then, a needy victim suffers in the event of a disaster.

God forbid that a disaster should occur. A faith-based organization would come to the aid of victims. And if history is consistent, some lobbying organization criticizes providing aid to the community and wants to restrict assistance. This lack of foresight is all because of selfish idealism at the expense of benefiting people. Furthermore, some jurisdictions would drag their feet because no money would be appropriated to disaster victims because they would not want to contribute to assistance alongside faith-based organizations. This is an honest observation of some jurisdictions' decisions based on their history of forbidding cooperation with people of all faiths.

National policy would remain in alignment with the Constitution if political representatives would discontinue promoting special interest groups' selfish ideologiesand consider benefiting the people. The real disaster is that certain members of lobbying organizations aren't honoring the Government by the people for the people.

It is imperative to note that homosexuality is a volatile mental condition (debased mind). The Bible reveals to us that homosexuals use physical force to preserve their perverted, mental perception of life. Genesis 19:9: *Again they said, "Stand back!" Then they said, "This one came in to stay here, and he keeps acting as a judge; now we will deal worse with you than with them." So they pressed hard against the man Lot, and came near to break down the door.* Again, prayer for protection of Christ's church and your family is of utmost importance. Like a cornered animal, when the true nature of homosexuality is publicly revealed as in the past, homosexuality is more openly violent. It's homosexuality's nature. It's known from current affairs; lying is homosexuality's way into public acceptance to continue abuse. Christianity needs to be dynamic in perception of the current homosexual deception because deception is the nature of homosexuals. When a homosexual is caught in a lie, false accusation of prejudice is the defense misdirecting the focus from unnatural homosexual behavior.

For homosexuals, endless lies are their only means of survival. Homosexuals are not benign because of their unwillingness to resign themselves to the fact that traditional marriage is the vital Constitutional institution. Amiableness and kindness are human characteristics and are not indicative of homosexual behaviors specifically when they are abusive. 2 Corinthians 11.14: *And no wonder! Satan himself transforms himself into an angel of light.* Homosexuals' adverse influences on our society are reversible with God's deliverance of homosexual victims from the power of darkness.

Some homosexuals are victims of abuse, but some are instigators of oppression. Not every homosexual is an abuser. One of the people deceived in the lustful activity is a victim. Jesus' foreknowledge of the resurrection reveals some homosexual victims' deliverance from abusers in Luke 17.34-35: *"I tell you, in that night there will be two* men *in one bed: the one will be taken and the other will be left. Two* women *will be grinding together: the one will be taken and the other left."* God's work still needs to done, but He is merciful to these two victims of homosexual abuse. In continuation of the proactive presentation of Laws of Nature and Nature's God, one man is compromised yet caught away with the Lord. Likewise, one woman is homosexually abused yet caught away with the Lord. With God, all things are possible.

It's exhausting to tolerate homosexuals' lies, perverse laws and violence. Genesis 19.15-16: *When the morning dawned, the angels urged Lot to hurry, saying, "Arise, take your wife and your two daughters who are here, lest you be consumed in the punishment of the city." And while he lingered, the men took hold of his hand, his wife's hand, and the hands of his two daughters, the Lord being merciful to him, and they brought him out and set him outside the city.* Lot's lethargy is parallel to some of today's Christians. Matthew 24.24: *"For false christs and false prophets will rise and show great signs and wonders to deceive, if possible, even the elect."* Although unacceptable behavior at the time of this writing, a committed homosexual relationship is considered tolerable behavior for a certain church's pastor, publicized nationwide. It's time to preach to the choir. Lot, attempting to reason with the homosexuals, offers his two daughters in Genesis 19.8 as an alternative to molesting the two angels abiding in his home. As evident in Genesis 19.9, the homosexual mob retaliates with unreasonable threats and violent behavior to an alternative.

Homosexuals viciously threatened lawsuits instilling fear, oh my! Lest we forget over the last four decades, outlandish homosexuals' rights demands have paralyzed our society including the APA in the 70s. We've all been caught off guard through the not so precocious conclusion that sophistication includes rejecting approximately 234 years of Constitutional wisdom concerning what's natural, and what's not?

The wrap when homosexuals threatened prejudicial lawsuits instigated the perverted humanitarianism that was accepted during the 1990s. It apparently made sense to falsely accuse innocent people of prejudice fulfilling homosexuality's demeaning agenda. Tolerance gained momentum to relieve private citizens from the annoyance of homosexuality's prejudiced legal allegations. But, what has been the price?

Threat of a prejudicial lawsuits from a strange homosexual, it's difficult to recall. Because homosexuality primarily targets uninformed institutions, organizations and businesses, it's easier to suppress the thought that homosexuality has been intimidating individual American's for decades.

Constitutionally, natural and political issues aren't currently evidencing much restoration. Homosexuals are riding along in the wake of alleged prejudicial lawsuits. People are still afraid to say, "homosexuality is unnatural" because they are afraid of lawsuits. What the people need are legislative confirmations that unnatural sexual behaviors are unconstitutional, and the perpetrators of unnatural sexual behaviors have no right to prosecute on the grounds of prejudiced that oppose the Constitution.

Partial statistics are quite frequently misappropriated, overrated and misconstrued. When special interest groups want to prove their point, they "squeeze blood out of a turnip." Legislative concessions (pork) are the political ramifications that are currently hampering our every day way of life. As a culture, we are now all victims of the homosexual subculture.

Not long ago as expounded in Chapter Three, homosexuality was diagnosed as a psychiatric medical disease. The psychiatric medical community refused to analyze and publicly acknowledge the origins of homosexuality under duress. But, homosexuality has been confirmed as an unconstitutional political issue. Constitutionally speaking, a homosexual relationship's ignorance of extinction speaks volumes to its inability to parallel traditional marriage. A same-sex union lacks providence revealing denial of its eminent outcome.

As long as public educators, psychiatric physicians and political representatives concur with the *US Constitution*, they have a consensus with people to maintain the natural freedom ordained in the Constitution. Self-evident facts do not require substantiation from so-called "experts" in education, medicine or politics. Only provident statistics are prudent in the light of letting the *US Constitution's* true freedom reign.

Chapter 5
Constitutional Cultures and Subcultures

Some subcultures possess detrimental traits that distinctly preclude their populations' behaviors from American citizens' unalienable rights. Examples of some of America's subcultures with members of the population that are oblivious victims follow: drug, entertainment (mass media), financial and homosexual subcultures. Collectively, exploitative subcultures instigate acts of legislation that are divisive to a healthy society.

Subcultures' illegal and unethical practices are also destructive to a productive culture. Intentionally or ignorantly, subcultures most often attempt to gain legal approval of their members' counterproductive detriments. Usually, lobbying groups propose legislation under the guise of liberty as seen in 2 Peter 2.19: *While they promise them liberty, they themselves are slaves of corruption; for by whom a person is overcome, by him also is he brought into bondage.*

What follows is an excerpt from Alexander Hamilton's introductory letter in support of the ratification of the *US Constitution* to national newspapers recorded in the *Federalist Papers*: "It will be forgotten, on the one hand, that jealousy is the usual concomitant of violent love, and that the noble enthusiasm of liberty is too apt to be infected with a spirit of narrow and illiberal distrust. On the other hand, it will be equally forgotten, that the vigor of government is essential to the security of liberty; that in the contemplation of a sound and well-informed judgment, their interests can never be separated; and that a dangerous ambition more often lurks behind the specious mask of zeal for the rights of the people than under the forbidding appearance of zeal for the firmness and efficiency of government."

The drug subculture instigates homosexual prostitution and tax evasion. The objective of the drug subculture most often does not benefit from political lobbying for legalization of recreational drugs except possibly current "Medical Marijuana" legislation.

America exemplifies an entertainment influenced society. When a celebrity paints a destructive homosexual subculture's trait as a Constitutional liberty, an illiberal idea has the potential to philosophically influence the masses.

The "S&L Scandal" and "Bank Bailouts" are examples of the financial subculture's detriments. Bets against the odds deny the long-term costs of homosexuality on the American culture for short-term profit at the expense of consumers.

A homosexual lobbying group pursues legislation for example same-sex marriage to alter the main cultures' perception of liberty. Instead of identifying same-sex marriage as destructive, homosexuality inappropriately denies its abuse declaring homosexual abuse the pursuit of happiness.

So, subcultures in America in many instances are destructive. Subcultural entanglements present a culturally acceptable facade. Because the entertainment, drug, financial and homosexual subcultures are in many cases philosophically united, these subcultures are narrowly unified in their homosexual lobbying efforts to rewrite the *US Constitution*. Subcultures misconstrue Constitutional liberty denying the Constitution's separate and equal station from subcultures' destructive detriments.

The United States has freedom with restriction. One of the freedoms is the freedom of speech. Life-threatening communication restricts free expression of an opinion. Homosexuality's fruitless occurrence threatens extinction, and consciously or unconsciously is the indicator of a destructive motive. The subtlety of destruction often presents itself under the guise of openness and freedom.

Declaring transparency or openness is not a license for legislation. Describing legislation as open indicates that the proposed legislation possibly has an existing perception of being illegal. Challenging existing law to formulate an alternate perception most often results in an unnatural legal premise. Overturning an illegal legislation places undue need to substantiate a restriction that should have excluded the proposal in the first place. While openness is the only substantiation for proposed illegal legislation, the accusation of prejudice diverts justification from the proposal limiting a well-informed discussion to consider the proposal.

The purposes of the US Government's Branches (Executive—administrate, Legislative—propose policy and Judicial—enforce) guard against the institution of unnatural government branches; while, open political policies (branches of government without parameters) ignore the Laws of Nature and Nature's God and leave a nation vulnerable. Political and natural considerations result in "a decent respect of the opinions of mankind," written in the *Declaration of Independence*. Respectful opinions declare that unnatural political acts of legislation are unconstitutional because unnatural acts of legislation are detrimental for our entire culture.

The United States Government's Structure illustrates God's (the Creator's) relationship with His people, the people's cultures in relationship to the Branches of Government and an individual's subcultural relationship(s) to the people's culture(s).

Key points of consideration follow for the United States Government's Structure.

The United States Government's Structure:

- The Branches of the United States Government are instituted among Men (People) and derive their just powers from the consent of the governed (voters).
- The People have an equal voice with the Executive, Legislative, and Judicial Branches of Government.
- The People's Constitutional cultures encompass Race, Color, Creed and National Origin.
- Subcultures of People: In direct correspondence to a subculture's provident unalienable attributes or destructive traits of animosity, a subculture's activity identifies it as either Constitutional or unconstitutional in nature.
- Aristocratic, influential or credulous classes of people quite often are a member of more than one subculture.
- Example of Subcultures: Education, Entertainment, Financial, Drug, Homosexual, Medical, Political and Religious.

As previously expounded, the homosexual subculture is destructive in a much more subtle way. Because a homosexual relationship is unnatural and unable to produce progeny, a homosexual relationship is not entitled to the marriage right. The acceptance of homosexuality's destructive traits in other subcultures compounds homosexuality's detriments.

It is axiomatic that the homosexual subculture has relationships or unconstitutional entanglements with other subcultures or cultures. It's time to correctly label the homosexual subculture's nature as "destructive" or "unconstitutional" Yes, the homosexual subculture exhibits humane traits because homosexuals are human, too. But, homosexuality's inherent trait that threatens the people's common welfare overwhelmingly contributes to the homosexual subculture's "destructive" description.

Race, color, creed and national origin include subcultures that are either beneficial or detrimental to the human culture's existence. Homosexuality's detriments and inherent inability to produce progeny preclude them from being a culture. However, homosexual people belong to a one or more human cultures.

We all belong to one or more subcultures. A subculture's contributions or detriments determine if the group honors the common good of the people or not. Contributions include provisional time for well-informed judgments that respect providence and expose destruction. Detriments include undermining our freedom without well-informed judgment. For example, misappropriations categorizing sexual orientation as a culture instead of a subculture defy the Constitution.

Some affluent homosexuals make major, financial contributions to lobbyists in an effort to revise the Constitution to include sexual orientation as a culture among the human cultures of race, color, creed and national origin. Also, charitable contributions from the subculture's affluent homosexuals does not categorically elevate a subculture to cultural status. Homosexuals' benevolent behaviors are more characteristic of their financial subculture than traits of the homosexual subculture.

Homosexuals are not a culture of people because their sexual behaviors are their priority and not human nature's preservation. Like liars, their behaviors are unacceptable because their behaviors do not nurture trust but deception. For example, homosexual support groups condone premature education of homosexual behavior addressing children below the age of consensual sex. Additionally, politicians that condone homosexual legislation do not truly express homosexuality's detriments.

Misrepresenting (lying) is a false account of a person's actions. Although, lying primarily misrepresents previous actions after the fact. Future actions may be given as an account to further perpetuate a lie. Lying is intrinsically bound to homosexuality. In that, a homosexual persistently rationalizes unacceptable behavior and vocalizes false assumption.

The equal opportunity to behave unacceptably is not a Constitutional right. In fact, protecting the people from unacceptable (destructive) behavior is clearly addressed in the *Declaration of Independence*.

Victims

Accusation that the Continental Congress gathered under duress is ill founded. The *Declaration of Independence* is a timeless document of freedom, but untimely criticism of the Founding Fathers is without merit. The intent of the members of the Continental Congress is recorded in the *Declaration of Independence* and follows: "And for the support of this Declaration, with a firm reliance on the protection of divine Providence, we mutually pledge to each other our Lives, our Fortunes and our sacred Honor." Self-evidence isn't arbitrary. However when it comes to a subculture expressing discontent, a special interest group attempts to redefine the Constitution to inordinately substantiate its own unconstitutional pursuit of happiness.

The Laws of Nature and Nature's God are non-destructive and invite provident consideration. Destructive and ignorant perceptions of the Constitution's self-evidence are contrary to the Constitution. Thus, the following conclusions are Constitutional: "A person isn't born homosexual, and God didn't make a person homosexual!" According to the *Declaration of Independence*, "all men are created equal." The words, "all men" pertain to all humankind.

Did God create people either heterosexual or homosexual? It has been a commonly held Christian belief that God had two choices, but it wasn't heterosexual or homosexual. Genesis 1.27: *So God created man in His own image; in the image of God He created him; male and female He created them.* No one was born homosexual. We were born either male or female.

God definitely designed men and women to complement each other. God created humankind in His own image. Genesis 2.24 *Therefore a man shall leave his father and mother and be joined to his wife, and they shall become one flesh.* As the Creator of humankind, God gave us simple guidelines. When a homosexual usurped God's design concerning human compatibility, an erroneous conclusion exalted personal opinion above the Word of God which was idolatrous. God didn't create or make a homosexual that way." Inordinately, a homosexual contrived an opinion about what God said to justify that homosexual's lapse in judgment.

Regretfully, a Christian who is not a homosexual is not immune to this deception believing this lie that God made homosexuals the way that they are. If God wants men or women to act differently, He ought to say so. Right? If God doesn't want homosexuals to be a homosexual, let Him tell that to people. Okay, God confirms what He said in Genesis 2.24 and Ephesians 5.31. God speaks to us in the Word of God (the Bible). Old Testament or New Testament, God's Word has the same message concerning homosexuality. Time changes. But, at this time, God's will for men and women is not going to change concerning marriage and the couple's sexual relationship. However, God does reveal to us when marriage between a man and a woman will no longer be the same in Matthew 22.30 and follows: *For in the resurrection they neither marry nor are given in marriage, but are like angels of God in heaven.*

"We hold these truths to be self-evident that all men are created equal," "the Laws of Nature and Nature's God" and "the separate and equal station" are Constitutional rights declaring independence from destructive alternatives. Regretfully, some rare and unnatural causes are evident in birth defects. Unnatural human occurrences are confirmation to refrain from unnatural exposure especially acceptance of homosexuality. Constitutionally, unnatural exposures to homosexuality hurt the human body.

God is able to cleanse us from all unrighteousness and purge our sins to restore the human body, soul and spirit. If you need God's cleansing from unnatural homosexual abuse, God confirms His faithfulness in 1 John 1.9: *If we confess our sins, He is faithful and just to forgive us our sins and to cleanse us from all unrighteousness.* God wants people to remain safe and enables us to overcome unnatural human occurrences.

As a Christian, a person needs to pray for God's healing to supersede all unnatural causes. If the unnatural confronts you, God has sent His Son for your healing. I Peter 2.24: *Who Himself bore our sins in His own body on the tree, that we, having died to sins, might live for righteousness—by whose stripes you were healed.* Please prioritize time for God in your personal life to pray for deliverance from the unnatural influence of destructive subcultures for yourself and others. The adverse affect of unnatural subcultures is temporal, and you are not bound by the illusion of worldly desires. God is greater as 1 John 4.4 reads, *You are of God, little children, and have overcome them, because He who is in you is greater than he who is in the world.*

Homosexuality's lapse in judgment tends to overflow infiltrating other institutional administrative decisions. For instance, public education's inhumane position on homosexuality effects financial misappropriations. Public education exhibits detrimental traits classifying it in its own subculture because of coercion.

Public education's administrators criticize taxpayer's scrutiny to metaphorically "shiny new buildings." While, taxpayers are already contributing to education's facilities maintenance for quality education. Taxpayers in many school districts support supplemental requests. People may recall many examples. For instance, new energy-efficient windows are a viable request to keep students warm and save on the cost of energy. Even though in many instances, adequate facility maintenance already has financial appropriations through taxpayers' support. Is impartiality even possible with so-called "independent education agencies?"

When public education's position on new facilities needs reinforcement, it suggests supporting documentation. For example, James E. Ryden's August 2009 article "All children deserve quality curriculum and schools" was published in *American School and University* (ASU). ASU is an education facilities magazine. James E. Ryden is ASU's Facility Planning columnist and an architect. Mr. Ryden's reference to academic testing scores is conducted through the Carnegie Foundation.

The following historical excerpts are from Carnegie Foundation's www.carnegiefoundation.org website: "In our first several decades, influential Foundation achievements included—the founding of the Educational Testing Service, and the creation of the Teachers Insurance Annuity Association of America (TIAA-CREF)....More recently, the Foundation's work focused on moral, civic and political education. The Foundation continues to work with community colleges to improve basic skills education in that sector."

As former students, some of us have remembered what educational testing meant. pencil-sores and all. But, today's academic testing standards have focused on moral, civic and political education. With consensus, educators' commentaries most often have lauded "moral, civic and political education" instead of traditional educational testing. Consequences have indicated that morality has been redefined, civic duty has instigated unnatural legislation and political education has impeded potential for children to learn. Immorality, homosexual support groups and illiteracy have escalated in an oppressive "brick 'n mortar" curricula.

Now documented among the destructive subcultures, the education subculture escalates. If it was not for the education subculture, the homosexual subculture would not be incorrectly assessed as a culture. Like the drug, mass media (entertainment) and financial subcultures, a superficial benefit is apparent and not a provident benefit. Sadly, further instigation of public education's misappropriations sacrifices the perception of children for the short-term solace of some people who belong to the homosexual subculture.

Public education's decent and respectful opinions of the *Declaration of Independence* and the *Constitution of the United States* previously inspired other nations of the world. The US Government's history and legacy were admired as a governing philosophy to emulate in order to reap the benefits of freedom. In our Nation, public education's administrators inappropriately reciprocated and embraced some of the detrimental qualities of other country's subcultures. These administrators tolerated world-views from outside of our Nation's borders and misinterpreted destructive lifestyle choices to be synonymous with compromising our free government.

When a person from another country visits our Nation as a guest, the person needs to acclimate to different surroundings. Even within our Country, a US citizen may experience culture shock while traveling to other regions. Although, culture shock is a misnomer. Instead of "culture shock," "subculture shock" is a more meaningful description of unnatural destructive behavior because a person is rarely in shock from observation of a different language, skin pigment and hair color. Moreover, subcultural behavior or subclass behavior when destructive startles a person.

Now, subculture shock is evident in our Country's cities. It's because the traditional wisdom of our Constitution is somehow questioned through so-called "progressive" yet transient causes. Even though, the decent respect for our Constitutional culture is what made us the strongest nation in the world. And now, it's normal to be shocked from the transient pursuit of legislation that does not secure the blessings of liberty to ourselves and our posterity.

Alienation occurs against citizens of the US while experiencing contradictions to the American culture. For example since the 90s, the Head Start program as part of its preschool curriculum commonly includes psychiatric assessment, sexual orientation and gender identification. If it's no big deal then eliminate these adult subjects from Head Start. A child below the age of five is certainly below the age of consensual sex and does not need to be confronted with overwhelming subjects. To illustrate the insurmountable ability for a child to assimilate adult subjects, it's time to examine the rudiment of learning like mathematics.

Identifying numbers and counting are foundational concepts to progress in learning during preschool. Addition, subtraction, multiplication and division are normally elementary school subjects. Although Algebra, Geometry, Trigonometry and Calculus have an some introduction in elementary education, advanced mathematics' skills are normally developed in the middle school and high school curriculum. Mathematics' theories are expounded in college above high school mathematics. Mathematics' practical applications are applied when people balance their checkbook and live with in a their means. Are preschool children to balance their checkbooks and budget? Children barely know how to responsibly exchange currency. Adults' tasks include balancing a checkbook and living within their means.

Public education and sexual education are confused concerning what andragogy and pedagogy are.

If a child spends his or her allowance foolishly, the results may be evident in a stomach ache from candy. If a child foolishly implements sexuality, active sex is life-altering. A premature sexual experience is overwhelming in the wake of the increases in venereal disease, unplanned pregnancy or homosexual abuse. Sexual education gloats concerning its privilege and denies its responsibility concerning ineffective sexual instruction.

In comparison, ought a preschool instructor confront preschool children with the question, "Do you like boys or girls?" It's apparent that educators are unable to recognize the natural progression of sexuality with the introduction of mature subjects in preschool and elementary education. Sexual orientation is a phrase with two parts neither of which an immature child ought to have responsibility to identify with dignity. Sexual implies an act that prepubescent children have no need to understand or practice, and an abstract or illustrated explanation is impertinent for inclusion in preschool instruction material. A child who is not physically and financially able to perform sex responsibly certainly is not emotionally able to comprehend compatibility. Procreation is a frequently abandoned term in public education because it references the Constitution's Laws of Nature and Nature's God. Public education in the sexual orientation curricula unnaturally ignores the emotional, financial and physical development of children. Additionally, no educator has the Constitutional right to call attention to a child's undeveloped sexual organs (private parts).

A Constitutional approach that respects a child's innocence follows:

- You were born a boy, or you were born a girl.
- Girls go in this restroom; boys go in the other restroom.
- Bullying a girl or boy is unacceptable.
- Boys do not play contact sports with girls. Girls do not play contact sports with boys.
- It is unacceptable to make fun of girls or boys because of their physical development.
- Boys or girls are not allowed to disrespectfully laugh, name-call or physically hit.
- No pushing, shoving or inappropriate touching to respect the child's space.
- If a child expresses that another child is too close, move away.
- Then when children reach the average age of consensual sex, public education forfeits the privilege of presenting procreation because sexual educators have collectively failed to present sexuality in a responsible manner.

Public sexual education courses have been primary contributors to the casual sexual attitudes of young adults. Irresponsible attitudes have been introduced, promoted and encouraged. Newspaper articles across our Country have reported the escalating increase of sexual activity with children below the age of consensual sex. Teenage casual sex couples have not been responsibly educated. Unacceptably, approximately fifty percent of children have been born to couples that have not been married. These have been devastating alternative attitudes considering about ten years ago the percentage of children born to unmarried couples was approximately twenty percent.

Self-evident truths are expounded in Luke 16.10 and follow: *"He who is faithful in* what is *least is faithful also in much; and he who is unjust in* what is *least is unjust also in much."* To elaborate on education's irresponsibility, educators have not admitted to contributing to the problem or overstepping their sexual education methods. Public education's administrators have been good at accusing parents or the media. Public educators have been insistent that they were an organization qualified to educate children about sexuality So if the primary educators of sexual education have not taken some responsibility for the sexual actions of the students, do children? Ineffective sexual instructions have been evident. Alternative sexual attitudes have been totally unacceptable.

The death of our Constitutional culture in public education is a time of grief. When I look in the eyes of a previously innocent child, I still see a glimmer of hope that someone will help. God knows children aren't receiving comprehensive education in public education. It's an alternative that is promoted against nature. Restoration is needed in public education that embraces traditional values like the *US Constitution*.

Subcultures, like the drug, mass media (entertainment), financial and homosexual are rarely accessible to the public as much as the public education subculture. Constitutional premises ought to be rudimentary for public education. Educational institutions need to reestablish the fundamental integrity of the Constitution as a pillar of our Government and not a detriment to freedom.

For example: Identifying an innocuous attribute of a Constitutional creed is a Constitutional aspiration for public education's curricula. Disrespect of the opinions of mankind alienates a religious organization's station into a destructive subculture. A creed's innocuous human factor Constitutionally protects a religion's participants. It's axiomatic that a creed without animosity is the only creed protected under the *US Constitution*. A respectful religion's self defense is often incorrectly assessed as barbarous, or a barbarous religion's assault is often incorrectly assessed as a religion's self defense. To dispel confusion, the *Declaration of Independence* lists examples of liberty and barbarism. No gray-area exists for those who accept the self-evident premises in the *Declaration of Independence* and the *US Constitution*. Other than providing for the common defense, any religious activity that impedes the propagation of the human race is unconstitutional.

Chapter 6
Above Compound English's Nomenclature

My granddaughter has expressed her curiosity when I've composed on the computer. She has reminded me many times of the simplicity of life. I have learned as much if not more from her than she's learned from me. While typing on the computer, my granddaughter has pointed at images on the monitor and peripheral device and has asked questions. One such day, she asked, "What is that grandpa?" Reluctantly, I replied, "A mouse." She laughed and said, "That's not a mouse." Oh— out of the mouths of babes!

On a previous day, I explained an icon which was far from a sacred image. To separate fact from fiction, I gently told her that it was an image that when selected with the pointer allows a person to do different things on the computer. The proper use of the word "icon" which was sacred has been attacked to put it lightly. This interaction made me recall my reconciliation to maintain my faculties above a computer's terminology.

The computer industry represents a class or subclass of people within the Mass Media (Entertainment) subculture. However the computer industry's detrimental nomenclature not only dominates the mass media subculture, computer jargon now compounds the English language and negatively influences the American culture. Because of an entanglement with the mass media subculture, the homosexual subculture deploys misnomers to justify homosexual legislation. "So, where is the English language's monitor (word police)?"

The English language was comprised of approximately 500,000 words in 1975 as documented a variety of literary websites. The number of English has doubled. According to the Global Language Monitor's www.globallanguagemonitor.com website, the English language has escalated to over 1,000,000 words. Compounded, what has been compromised?

From wizards to worms, the slang terms associated with computer use have inundated our language. Slang technology terms have altered the meaning of existing English words. When a language doubles in size in a in a time-span of approximately 35 years, the existing words of the language are compromised.

The disadvantages of compounding the English language have been unanticipated. The rules for computer terminology to comply with the English language have been ignored. Word associations of the dictionary meanings of words with computer jargon have revolting contradictions, and people have compromised their perception as a result.

All of the literary heroes that have inspired us before compound English have not affected the English language as much as the last 35 years of computer marketing terminology. Now, the nuances of our English language have been disregarded as insignificant to the perpetrators. Have average people been misdirected to prioritize a so-called "computer virus" over an inconsiderate naming convention's corruption of the English language?

"Computer-friendly" has been attributed as one of the over 500,000 new words or phrases in the English language. I was taught in elementary school that an inanimate object can not be friendly. What has been friendly about a computer? A misnomer like computer-friendly has been the norm instead of the exception. Computer-friendly actually has appeared in some dictionaries. A more appropriate term for computer-friendly would have been human-activated or operator-frustrated. Historically, a new meaningful term has been described with respect to commonly accepted words. Right?

The origins of the English language were primarily derived from Latin, Greek and languages derived from the same. The Romance Languages adhered to the distinction between a human and an object sacred. Previously, slang terms quite often were not cited in dictionaries. Drawbacks to compound English have indicated that computers have been elevated to the level of human characteristics, and humans have been degraded to the level of computer processes. Examples like "computer programming languages" and "computer users" have intimidated people and escalated a computer.

When I referred to a computer programming language as one of many computer programming versions while attending college, the instructor replied, "What are you talking about?" What had made sense to me certainly wasn't acceptable to the instructor. A living being communicated with a language. A computer implemented a myriad of zeros and ones and evolved into not much more than a preoccupied integration of time-consuming computer programs. Hey, that was not very computer-friendly!

Terms like chip, favorite and menu have been assigned new meanings in our language. But, where were the "word police?" When I was in elementary school, the teachers monitored the correct usage of the English language. Slang was not accepted conversation in school. Now, teachers have simply followed the indiscriminate curricula. Moreover, the administrators over the public education curricula have not encouraged enough correction of contrary terminology. Therefore, they have been confounded. Would they have offended a computer with a little scrutiny?

Computer technology is not magic or wizardry. It's just computer programs, circuits and the rest. Embracing contrary language as being somehow meaningful increases the current confusion in the English language.

Will we continue to allow computer nomenclature's influence on the English language? To say, "We are victims of computer slang" is an understatement. Unless we resolve the inconsiderate use of compound English, our culture is sure to continue being compromised.

Like an audience at a magic show, we all are impressed with the graphical user interface. Our priorities are distracted from the dysfunctional names attributed to computer technology's disregard for the English language. We continue being distracted, but resolutions for the confusion aren't addressed. Previously, words being added to the dictionary needed to follow the rules. The computer naming convention has defined its basis as being "meaningful" but breaks most of the rules.

The following information was extracted from the keyword search of "GUI" at Wikopedia's en.wikipedia.org/wiki/Graphical_user_interface web address: Douglas C. Englebart developed the first graphical user interface (GUI) between 1963-1965. Although, Xerox Corporation refined and extended hyperlinks to the GUI in the 70s. Atari Inc. produced video arcade games from 1972-1984. Apple Computers was accredited with the first successful marketing of the personal computer.

The GUI's application terminology delinquently eroded in gaming. Gaming's slang terminology traversed to personal computers and degraded an English word as simple as "personal" which violated personal privacy.

Whether you agree with the million word count or not, many foreign countries consider English the mongrel language and repel the acceptance of English words. Instead, they prefer to evaluate slang computer terms and use more appropriate terminology from their various cultures. In the past, the British found the colonies' disregard for English repulsive. Previously, the British rejected American attacks on the English language with phrase like "Let's roundup the doggies while trailblazing out West." But, the British are clicking their mice navigating the Internet.

Redefining an everyday term has confused English's basic foundation for all of us. The merit of meaningful words that meet true standards has been underemphasized. Now, it has been necessary to examine the compound English that we have accepted.

Ideally, public education ought to resume its role as the "word police." Honor for human existence over a computer could respect English in conversation and writing. A fully comprehensive English Appreciation course would rectify the understanding of some of the over 500,000 words that we incorrectly accept. A constructive term could replace a corrupted term. A comprehensive textbook could accurately address the necessity to distinguish between human characteristics and computer processes. A course such as this could reverse some of the negative effects of compound English. Is this too optimistic?

If children are not able to distinguish respect for human nature over operating a computer, ought children have the option of operating a computer? The hazards of operating a computer are numerous and long-lasting. Computer usage needs more of an introduction than just knowing how to type on a keyboard. Our culture is now experiencing cyberbullying, identity theft and more exploitation because we have not anticipated the drawbacks of intimidated and uninitiated computer operators.

Breaking the rules and accepting compound English indicate contagious complacency. Destructive subcultures contribute to the compound English language with blind acceptance. Unless we accept the degraded meaning of the 500,000 new words in the English language, precariously, we are not viewed as "politically correct" people. The questions are: "What is correct about politics, and what have politicians done correctly?" But, accepting misnomers like "politically correct" and "computer-friendly" are virtually unchallenged.

Victims

A person might say, "Get over it." It is difficult being complacent. History holds the people responsible for monitoring the English language. Will the English language once again be scrutinized?

Zeros and ones remain the building blocks of the graphical user interface. The principles of positive and negative are a universal law that we all utilize in order to take advantage of the newest technology. Numeric electrical currents are buried deep in our computers' operating systems, although, images on the monitor appear to have many hues?

The meaning of the word "positive" is now considered subjective. In practical application, this type of computer programming would draw a blank screen on our computers.

Why hasn't computer technology saved us money? Just fifteen years ago, the business in which I worked as a manager employed approximately 24 experts that were lovingly referred to as the "secretarial pool." Each expert was efficient and analyzed the documentation for a division of the retail business. When PCs gained momentum, it was thought that automatic reports would provide the required documentation without the payroll costs. After laying off the experts, one day, the auditor arrived. The auditor inquired, but no one was able to reconcile the reports or answer the auditors inquiries. The auditor placed the facility on probation. The business was given six months to accumulate the expert knowledge in order to responsibly present the business' accountability.

The auditor returned after the probation period. The expert knowledge in order to present each division's documentation had not been acquired. The auditor had relied on the secretarial pools' experts to organize and present reports for each division's accountability. Just like, the business relied on the experts to monitor each division's compliance. It was not the auditor's responsibility to maintain compliance and alerting each division concerning discrepancies. The responsibility shifted to a newly appointed compliance officer who shifted the responsibility to the store manager. The store manager shifted the responsibility to the department manager. When the department manager focused responsibility on the audit requirements, the department's sales-floor wasn't monitored because the priority shifted to justifying the reports. Now semi-experts in the department's audit requirements, the department manager's focus was divided, and sales never recovered. The business failed and closed its doors.

Tim G. Riley

Accountability confirms a business' viability to support the internal expenses (salaries), external expenses (bills) and provide a product or service. The difference between earning a living and making money resides on a Constitutional foundation. When the credit card interest rate is 20 times the average interest on passbook savings, establishing commerce doesn't appear to proportionately balance expenses with service.

To what extent has a computer's nomenclature adversely effected the business industry? For one thing, accountability has been compromised. Declaring "accountability" when describing "unaccountability" has been evidenced with the digression from a responsible business practice. The expertise necessary for a business to monitor a division responsibly has not been properly assessed. Now, the business industry has abandoned the required expertise to perform responsibly. The "good enough" business philosophy has abandoned accountability under the guise of computers saving money.

Literally a "culture shock," the computer industry's guise of saving us money is bankrupting our Nation leaving us oblivious to treachery. A computer is unable to replace the human factor necessary to motivate and act accountable. Is the new business ethic to ignore accountability? Requiring the employment of the appropriate experts to again perform responsibly ought to be common business sense. With the acknowledgment of a computer's inability to communicate, an accountability expert has the ability to restore a business' respectability. It's a lie for a business to report its inability to employ accountability experts. The truth is our Nation needs to fine or prosecute irresponsible businesses that are not compliant to accountability.

If the wrong question is being asked or if the right question isn't being posed, denial of a computer's inability to save money reinforces the "good enough" philosophy. The arbitrary application of the "good enough" philosophy falls short of competent compliance to avoid accountability. "Good enough" may be more efficient when it comes to implementing a reusable paper clip instead of a disposable staple. But, when a business supervenes an unaccountable computer program instead of employing an accountable expert, conspiracy to circumvent accountability is evident.

The "good enough" philosophy is a product of so-called "empowering." When a business' administration discovered that a computer didn't save money and divided a functional worker's responsibilities, instead of abandoning an unaccountable computer's functions, empowering has increased a worker's responsibilities leaving the worker to rely on application support. Empowering increased a business' administration, operation and support costs while inhibiting accountability and effectiveness of a worker who is constantly attacked with more empowering.

A run-away computer's expense is preserved, so reassigning another task emulates change and progress. Total computer empowerment denies all accountability with the assumption that a business acts responsibly. As a tool, a computer processes input, but accountability requires a human expert. Does this sound familiar?

Currently so-called "financial experts" say, "A regular citizen simply doesn't understand the Financial Industry." Hearsay and conjecture are simply not facts. Financially corrupt institutions need to understand that borrowing money from a foreign country is not a write-off. Just like, overestimating market projections and relying on a computer reports are not practical since the "Bailout."

Continued corruption jeopardizes a financial institution's existence. This is not a lesson to be learned again the "really" hard way. A salary for a compliance expert(s) for accountability is a small price to pay compared to a government takeover for noncompliance. This is not a threat. It's a responsible business practice. The Federal Government also needs to realize that a computer is just a tool and is unable to replace a human being.

A destructive subculture rarely reforms its lack of accountability. Restoration is a deliberate process that adheres to provident standards that avarice refuses to implement. An instigator of corruption likes to invite others to tolerate unaccountability on the self-imposed destination to the abyss.

Moreover, thank you to the many people that uphold the integrity of our English language and operate a business responsibly. Honest assessment of accountability is essential to free enterprise and our Nation's security. Proverbs 25.11 reads: *A word fitly spoken* is like *apples of gold in settings of silver.*

PART 3
THE CREATOR'S MEANING OF THE PURSUIT OF HAPPINESS IN THE US CONSTITUTION

Precious words from a child's perspective, "We can be happy in the U' States' cause the Cr'ater gave us Justice for all. And, it's not 'structive (destructive) 'cause the third, big gift makes us Happy."

Chapter 7
Beyond Defensive to Proactive

The acid test that follows is solely an example that illustrates the instigation of a education's "equal access" mission to influence children. This scenario is self-evident with public education's mission and its entanglement with the homosexual subculture.

A communication to the school's faculty announces that each teacher has a conference scheduled with the principal. The nature of the conference pertains to the foundation for responding to questions from children. Measuring educational uniformity is the responsibility of the principal during the conference. With the assurance that each teacher is able to access a reference, the average teacher's academic achievement welcomes an education administrator's innocuous interaction.

The question the principal poses from the perspective of a child to each teacher follows: "Why is 'Prudence' so important in the *Declaration of Independence?*" Do you (the reader) hear a pregnant-pause? An honest assessment allows each teacher the opportunity to review the second paragraph of the *Declaration of Independence.* "Accordingly as all experience has shown," an average teacher relies on the current curriculum's philosophy seeking the approval of the peer-principal. Self-evidently, a teacher's ambiguous response more than likely defies the Founding Fathers' separation from light and transient causes. However honest, the inquiry defines the contradictory curriculum that a teacher currently represents.

This acid test reveals that public education overwhelmingly instigates tolerance of homosexuality. Each educator already knows the potential opposition from parents that a homosexual club's residence poses. Consequently, an educator evades elaboration of homosexuality's philosophical integration. An independent Internet search of a sexual orientation group's mission draws no distinction between targeting children in public or private education. Homosexuality's lobbying relentlessly instigates "equal access" legislation for all children below the age of consensual sex.

Currently in history, Christians have responded defensively to so-called "political correctness." Christians are falsely accused with the misnomer "homophobic." Christians have not feared homosexuals. If anything, they've advocated on the behalf of children for the preservation of human existence. On the other hand, homosexuals have disregarded human existence, and their destructive motives have been exposed.

The term homophobic implies that Christians do not want to help homosexuals which is simply not the case. With the Word of God, a Christian wants to help restore a homosexual's wholeness. To be proactive, a Christian needs to respond in a godly manner. Romans 12.17-18: *Repay no one evil for evil. Have regard for good things in the sight of all men. If it is possible, as much as depends on you, live peaceably with all men.* The phrase *Have regard for good things in the sight of all men* is translated *Provide things honest in the sight of all men* in the KJV translation of Romans 12.17. Right now, the Christian position on homosexuality isn't as unified as possible. Prudent communication exposes homosexuality's unnatural pursuits to politicians and reestablishes the Constitutional foundation to live peaceably with all men including homosexuals.

The following is a real-life example of the duress that a Christian is confronted with during a college admissions or job interview: "With this school's diverse (homosexual) population of students and teachers, do you have a problem with that?" What a loaded question! Homosexuality is nothing new. The real issue is in the mind of the interview's administrator. Because guilt wears on the mind of a homosexual, it is a question in the mind of the educator if the person ought to be teaching. Another example of an interviewer's inquiry follows, "Do you think a homosexual teacher has the right to teach?" My response is, "Why not?" But, what is it that the interviewer is really asking? The real question that is evident with education's instigation of homosexual tolerance follows: "Do you think that a homosexual teacher has the right to teach and promote homosexuality in the classroom?" The answer to that question is, "No!"

Homosexuals that refuse to accept the deliverance of the Word of God are the ones that need to defend their actions. High moral standards, God's standards and the common welfare's standards need credence in public education to prevent homosexual clubs from accessing children. Currently, homosexual clubs more often than not set the moral standards in public education. Sexual orientation groups that have access to K-12 children ought be able to answer this question: "How does your group stand on children below the age of consensual sex engaging in sexual activity?" "Kids will be kids, and children ought to feel open to physically express themselves" aren't the right answers. People with debased minds are incapable of providing a dignified response that exhibits restraint. Premeditated homosexual lies aren't eminent. Therefore because homosexuals are unable to communicate within the parameters of Constitutional law, prudent and provident responses are absent and disqualify homosexual teachers' abilities to effectively teach children. However, homosexual victims may be an exception. Homosexual victims' restorations of dignity and discipline reside in their commitment to oppose the perpetuation of homosexual abuse.

Public school teachers bear the future's burden through molding the minds of children. Acting upon the homosexual standard of the "Safe Schools" curricula, teachers hamper perception of the family unit. They are underestimating the importance of honestly educating children. Some children express their honest opinions. When educators say, "That's just your parents talking," teachers are undermining the family unit. Additional teachers' indiscretions include: "Your parents don't know everything, and that's old thinking." Adult issues concerning unnatural homosexuality have no merit for compromise in primary education and no place for promotion at all levels of education. Homosexuals' instigation and indiscretion of tolerance are infecting public education's curricula into accepting their perverted behavior as normal. Teachers need to support the family unit and not degrade it. Matthew 25.40 reveals: *And the King will answer and say to them, "Assuredly I say to you, inasmuch as you did not do it to the least of these My brethren, you did it to Me."* God takes this extremely personal.

The English language needs protection from corruption through actively acknowledging and confessing what the Word of God says. Even if everyone that you know home-schools their children, it's eminent for each person to personally resolve political correctness with God's guidance for Christ's church. What God thinks about homosexuals is not unrighteous judgment. It is the truth. Guidance to Christ's church may include encouraging, praying and writing local, state and federal political representatives. Please notice the following scripture doesn't limit prayer for people in our Country: 1 Timothy 2.1-2: *Therefore I exhort first of all that supplications, prayers, intercessions,* and *giving of thanks be made for all men. For kings and all who are in authority, that we may lead a quite and peaceable life in all godliness and reverence.* God is bigger than supreme rulers, judges and legislators. Therefore, He is able to answer this prayer request to preserve our freedom. Along with praying for your family and Christ's church, please add to your prayer list all people including political representatives and school administrators. Because worldly political correctness is an accepted philosophy in political and educational circles, consistent communication in combination with prayer acknowledges God. The Constitution's intention from its authors remains in the *Declaration of Independence* and follows: "with a firm reliance on the protection of divine Providence."

For us and our children, we continue to subject ourselves to be victims of the homosexual subculture to the extent that we allow a subculture to oppress our way of life. The phrase "political correctness" and its illiberal definition are an attack on the English language. Although, political correctness is currently an oxymoron, Christians' Constitutional rights allow us to clarify political correctness. Through clarification, Christians can make political correctness work to compliment the Constitution. Because political correctness literally needs provident clarification, Christians' references to political correctness can utilize the Constitution's excerpts declaring that homosexuals' rights are unconstitutional. Through God's knowledge and wisdom, we are able to address today's issue of homosexuality and daily renew our Lordship of Jesus. 2 Peter 1.3 *As His divine power has given to us all things that pertain to life and godliness, through the knowledge of Him who called us to glory and virtue.* God and His Word give us strength to act with a proactive resolution instead of defensively. God's promises allow us to appreciate the time we make to cherish His Word.

Currently and from the fall of humankind, the words of communication have been attacked and degraded. Romans 1.25: *Who exchanged the truth of God for the lie, and worshiped and served the creature rather than the Creator, who is blessed forever.* Idolatrous acts have exchanged the truth of God for a lie. We as believers in God have needed to be aware of the attacks on our language and have implemented a proactive resolution.

Making God's Word our own started when we confessed with our mouth the Lord Jesus as recorded in Romans 10.9. As believers, God gave us the answer to the attacks on language, so you or I are not overwhelmed. Ephesians 4.14-15: *That we should no longer be children, tossed to and fro and carried about with every wind of doctrine, by the trickery of men, in the cunning craftiness of deceitful plotting, but, speaking the truth in love, may grow up in all thing into Him who is the head—Christ.* So, identification of an attack and clarification of the truth restored the language at Ephesus and eliminated the confusion. From God's perspective, speaking the truth in love resolved the opposition's definition of political correctness.

Why are Christians put in the position to have to justify why homosexual clubs should not have access to children? Clearly, the people in homosexual clubs should be required to prove if they are worthy to be trusted with children before they ever have access to children.

Is a homosexual club required to:

- Provide any references for the people in its organization?
- Request approval from parents to access children?
- Verify credentials including its objectives?

Regretfully in public education, an obtrusive policy is the standard for homosexual clubs. Without provident consideration, public education misconstrues prejudice, dismisses justifiable inquisition and instigates unconditional acceptance of homosexuality.

A believer has the right to correct a verbal homosexual assault. In pubic and the work place, a believer needs to walk circumspectly with God's wisdom 2 Corinthians 10.5 states: *Casting down arguments and every high thing that exalts itself against the knowledge of God, bringing every thought into captivity to the obedience of Christ.* A wise course of action is to calmly acknowledge or state, "It's not natural, that's enough, or it's not acceptable for a person to violate your rights with a destructive conversation." And, it is not necessary for you to explain your response to avoid a shouting match. You may say what God works in your heart to say. It's good to keep on task. While upholding your rights, please avoid tangents thrown at your statement. Anyone who reads the *US Constitution* knows you have unalienable rights to life, liberty and the pursuit of happiness. And, anyone with a conscience knows that perverted attitudes are wrong. Thankfully in many states, public law still verifies the same. You have the freedom to expose homosexual abuse as unnatural, irresponsible and deceptive. That's what homosexual abuse is.

When a sexually oriented organization wants access to children who are below the age of consensual sex, the inference of the motives of the organization for access to children is predatory. For a so-called "Safe School" to consciously ignore predators is evidence of total deception. This conclusion is true whenever a group emulates the destructive nature of its organization. For example, a member of Alcoholics Anonymous needs to avoid bars. Then, why does a person in the homosexual club have access to K-12 children in public schools? It's not convincing to presume that a leader of the homosexual club is not sexual fanatic.

Children in various age ranges have various degrees of aptitude to determine the character of an adult or a child. Naturally, children require little to no degree of sexual knowledge. For educators to ignore these facts and allow homosexual clubs access to children is unconscionable. Homosexual clubs identify their members as straight (unlikely), bisexual (more likely), transgender, gay or lesbian. Then, are we so complacent to accept that homosexual clubs' motives are anything but sexual in nature? School administrators' tolerances of sexual orientation for children in public education are today's perverted priorities in public education. School administrators need to be accountable and not unnaturally mandate homosexuality's tolerance for children.

With God's help, the people of the United States can succeed in expelling homosexual clubs from public education. Homosexuality's rants already confirm their unnatural behavior. People who have ears to hear need to lovingly call attention to homosexuality's barbarism. Homosexuality's detriments disqualify its subculture from equal access in public education's curricula and mission.

Human tendency is to gloat. Therefore, it's important that a novice does not pursue a single-handed attempt to overcome the homosexual power of darkness. That's why God says in Ephesians 2.8-9: *For by grace you have been saved through faith, and that not of yourselves;* it is *the gift of God. Not of works lest anyone should boast.* It's important to fully realize that God gives us the victory because He loves us. The only reason that the victory isn't clear is because a consensus for Christians to clarify political correctness needs to be a priority.

Your posterity may not be enrolled in public education. Some other children need prayers and advocacy to restore comprehensive education standards as encouraged in Philippians 2.3-4: Let *nothing* be done *through selfish ambition or conceit, but in lowliness of mind let each esteem others better than himself. Let each of you look out not only for his own interests, but also on the interests of others.* Through written, telephone or face-to-face communication, we can reclaim traditional education for our posterity through political legislation. The Laws of Nature and Nature's God are politically correct legislation for the US Department of Education to implement in its curricula according to the *Declaration of Independence*.

I was acquainted with a man who had recently been married. He left the area shorty after I had met him to pursue his career. One day months after his departure, he called me on the telephone and asked if I would meet him. He had a question for me and sounded somewhat desperate. Being recently married, I thought that he had some questions about married life and agreed to meet him in a public place. The turmoil in his visage was apparent upon locating him. I greeted him, sat down and asked, "How may I be of assistance to you?" To my shock, he propositioned me for gay sex. I communicated to him what I had assumed that he might have some questions about married life. He persisted with advances. I brought to his attention that he needed God's help. With lust, he persisted. When I emphatically refused to discuss the insult further, he threatened me with the words, "I know where you live." With God's word of knowledge, I said, "And if you arrive at my home, the answer will still be the same—no!" Matthew 24.24: *For false christs and false prophets will rise and show great signs and wonders to deceive, if possible, even the elect.* Previously, I had no idea that this married man was a homosexual or bisexual.

The following deceptive steps are typical of a homosexual predator :

- Misrepresent a whimsical facade to gain a victim's trust.
- Falsely express the need for a victim's participation or help.
- Badger a victim to a location of the predator's choosing.
- Distort prejudice and the victim's trust in human nature.
- And if the victim concedes or not, threaten the victim.

It is extremely difficult for a person to walk in the way of the Lord practicing predatory deception. It is worth making the time to personally recall the similarities of Adam and Eve's seduction. Without Christ, the serpent's threat of eternal separation from God is real for every man, woman and child. God took away the sting of death in 1 Corinthians 15.57: *But thanks be to God who gives us the victory through our Lord Jesus Christ.*

Anxiety, frustration and oppression may be challenges facing people who attend your church. Remember, the debased minds of homosexuals begin with the idolatrous act of perverting the truth of God into a lie. Homosexuals twist legal terms founded on the Word of God in the *US Constitution* to promote their continued abuse of humankind.

The first line of proactive expression for Christians is to simply acknowledge and possibly state that what is being said is a lie—homosexuality is not natural after all. More often than not, it's better not to express anger. The destructive scheme of homosexuals is profoundly deceitful. Consequently when Christians try to compensate for potential abuse from homosexuals, worldly wisdom does not provide any solution.

Please emphasize to your congregation not to resort to the methods of the world for answers. This is not talking about civil letter writing. Libelous threat has no place in Christianity. In truth, that's why homosexuality in the United States is still an illegal act. Rightly so, people are still protected against homosexual abuse under the *US Constitution*.

Important elements for a letter to a politician primarily are initiated with prayer. Some people include their name, address, telephone number and e-mail address after the body of the letter without a letterhead. The political title with the politician's name, the political office and the address are entered before the date and greeting. The political representative's complete name and title are also essential. The political representative's responsible service and your gratitude of the representative's service are a recommendation in the introductory paragraph. Then, your political issues of concern are communicated in the paragraphs that follow. Your views motivate the political representative to complete reading your request with respectful and brief communication. In contrast, some political acts of legislation incite anger, but we as Christians must not succumb to inconsiderate political provocation. When our words are "seasoned with salt," the truths presented in the body of the letter are your point of communication and reflect only the common good. A reasonable length to your letter and clarity are often more important than covering all of the unconstitutional tactics of an issue.

Please consider some of the following elements for a letter to a politician:
Political Title With Politician's Full Name (for example: Senator John Doe)
Political Office (for example: US Senate)
Full Address
Date

Political Title With Politician's Full Name (for example: Senator John Doe):

Thank you for the care and consideration that you are communicating while serving. My prayers are with you and yours for strength to serve.

Please consider not supporting the proposed legislation to repeal of the "don't ask, don't tell" policy for the military. In reality, the "don't ask, don't tell" legislation has been in force for nearly 234 years. Historically, legislative wisdom implores us not to compromise for a short-term or an illiberal cause. The *Declaration of Independence's* political foundation follows: "Prudence, indeed, will dictate that Governments long established should not be changed for light and transient causes."

Thank you for making time to consider that same-sex relationships are limited to the participants' lifespans. As they are, homosexuals' self-imposing limitations oppose the Laws of Nature and Nature's God. Open acceptance and tolerance are counterproductive and condone unsolicited and unnatural propositions in the field of battle.

Sincerely,
Your Name

Full Address
Telephone
E-mail Address

Constitutionally prudent expression is proactive communicating thankfulness for the freedom endowed by our Creator. Taking away an unalienable right isn't Constitutional. A true right never violates the providence of another person. When a slave or other victim of oppression gains freedom, the pursuit of happiness ought not require a new citizen's tolerance of homosexual abuse. Does a parent send a child to school, so the child accepts unnatural behavior that results in human extinction? The "creed" of people is protected when God's love of no harm is the intent.

Race, color, creed and national origin are inherited family rights with ourselves and our posterity protected under the *US Constitution*. The unalienable rights endowed by our Creator do no harm to their neighbor including life, liberty and the pursuit of happiness.

Nature's God set up the law of love that it does no harm to a person's neighbor. The separation between sexual abuse and consensual homosexual sex occurs only in the minds of sexual predators. In fact, "consensual homosexual sex" is a misnomer because the consensual sex law was written to enforce the natural sexual relationship between a man and a woman that is not inherent in homosexuality. The lie concerning an impossible distinction between a sexual predator and a consensual homosexual partner evolves from tolerance to avoid accusation of prejudice. Preservation of human existence is the Constitutional precedence for concluding a consensual homosexual relationship is impossible. Regretfully, homosexual abuse effects the mind of its victim impairing the person's ability to distinguish between what's natural, and what's not?

Prayer, counseling and the Word of God are an effective course to restore victims of homosexual abuse. Victims with unresolved homosexual abuse find themselves at the precipice of accepting sexual abuse as normal or natural. Proactive devotion and provident consideration lead the way for our godly nature to protect our natural Constitutional rights.

Lies are exactly what our society needs to address. Because accepting homosexual abuse is an expensive medical treatment, victims may be further victimized by becoming a life-long pharmaceutical patients. Life-long prescription drugs are common for victims of unresolved homosexual abuse. Although, resolution and restoration from the issues of homosexual abuse may be therapeutically treated. In order to receive behavioral therapy treatments, identifying and verifying restorative practices are necessary to avoid destructive practices that tolerate homosexuality.

Because of the APA's removal of homosexuality as a psychiatric disorder, psychiatrists and psychotherapists are no longer required to publicly acknowledge victims of homosexual abuse in the previous manner. As you may recall, administrative psychiatrists and psychotherapists with the APA buckled under peer pressure in the 70s. Individual physicians and practitioners may be supportive of establishing a political stance against homosexuality but not the APA licensing board for now.

Please consider the following Constitutionally Correct and natural steps for resolution or restoration from homosexual abuse:

- Accept Creator's resolution or restoration from the Bible.
- Confirm counseling or medical practice's resolution or restoration.
- Victim describes a previous abuse not a person's present identity.
- Identify either the homosexual abuse or the homosexual abuser.
- Forgive the abuser and repudiate the abuse.
- Restrain the abusive or abuser's destructive nature.

Reasons to forgive an abuser and refuse to be subject to the homosexual abuse are apparent when an abused person realizes that the abuser was a victim of sexual abuse, too. Ephesians 4.32: *And be kind one to another, tenderhearted, forgiving one another, even as God in Christ forgave you.*

Forgiving an abuser may almost immediately occur. The forgiveness of an abuser is not to be confused with the refusal to forgive the abuse. Homosexual abuse is always wrong and never forgiven; it's Constitutionally unacceptable. Remorse on behalf of the abuser is not a mandatory condition for the victim to forgive.

A victim may need to ask God for forgiveness for an unwise decision including not listening to God. Honestly, a victim may regretfully be fellow-shipping with the wrong group of people, denying the motives of those people and justifying the same people's inconsiderate actions. A scripture for your consideration comes to mind in 2 Corinthians 6.14: *Do not be unequally yoked together with unbelievers. For what fellowship has righteousness with lawlessness? And what communion has light with darkness?* And when applied, God's love guards a victim from further abuse.

Confrontation of an abuser may overcome obstacles like time, environment and willingness to plan the confrontation. Confronting an abuser may take place many years after the abuse. The anger that accompanies abuse in many cases does not promote resolution in a confrontation. With the wrong time, place and motive as circumstances of the initial abuse, a confrontation's effectiveness coheres with the opposite conditions.

The wrong people, place and time instigate similar conditions for another abusive situation. Confrontations for homosexual abuse victims with their abusers need to take place under victims' natural terms. Therefore, homosexual victims are less likely to confront their abusers. Because homosexual abusers relentlessly deny victims their basic rights to human existence, unresolved crimes against humanity reside with the Creator for resolution.

In resolution and restoration, homosexuals have no substantiation that homosexuality has any merits because homosexual relationships are not natural. Public sexual education's exposures of adult sexual orientation to children below the age of consensual sex are unnatural. Sexual education has no axiomatic foundation to be in public education's curricula. Homosexual relationships are subcultural and not on the same cultural level as race, color, creed or national origin.

At the time of this writing, current schemes to legislate Public Health Care are another deception to misconstrue homosexual relationships as equal to natural marriages. Simultaneously, same-sex partners are allowed to claim marital status on the 2010 Census. Although costly, many private businesses already extend health insurance to employees' same-sex partners. However, most government agencies do not extend health insurance to employees' same-sex partners. "Health care for all?" Homosexual rights are unconstitutional because they violate unalienable rights. Let's not be naive if Public Health Care legislates more unconstitutional concessions.

Some American people are overly tolerant of unnatural relationships. People who choose relationships that are unable to produce offspring still have citizen's rights. But, why do relationships that are inherently unable to propagate children seek preferential rights? The Constitution's human rights outline the pursuit of happiness for ourselves and our posterity. Human relationships with the inherent potential to propagate clearly define the Constitutional institution concerning marital rights.

It's important to note: Public Health Care Reform without provident consideration attempts to hastily propose legislation including same-sex partners in one form or another. "Individual health insurance for all" is not the answer for any family especially not for a single parent. Individualizing health insurance proliferates the stigma that the Constitution is designed to cater to individuals.

Why isn't a declaration of sexual orientation required for insurance coverage? History is repeating itself. Accusation of prejudice attempts to intimidate, so a person tolerates homosexuality's manipulation. Subsidizing homosexuality's destructive behavior (health care) proliferates the cycle of homosexual abuse. In many respects, Public Health Care Reform is a guise to legislate financing expensive homosexual health care.

The words, "We the people," exemplify our common good. We are much more interdependent on each other than we're led to acknowledge. Our neighbors' appreciations for the American family may influence political representatives to avoid hasty unconstitutional legislation.

Historically, some legislators sacrifice timely consideration at the expense of families for individual rights. Yes—in our Constitutionally based society, individuals are all important but not at the expense of the common good. Economically, individuals frequently have more money to lobby for their individual issues. Why don't individuals extend some humanitarian consideration toward families for the common good?

If any current government health care agency had a short application to receive medical assistance, awareness of the government's propensity for bureaucracy wouldn't be prevalent. No health care form to complete is equally disturbing meaning your health care is predetermined. Will a healthy political debate provide a voice for the people?

This writing is not intended to advocate that individuals go without medical insurance. After all, isn't Medicare or Medicaid intended for individuals who need medical assistance?

Chapter 8
Axiomatic Laws of Nature and Nature's God

A bumper sticker caught my attention because of the illustration. A depiction of a fish was precariously combined with its tail fin peddling a bicycle. The slogan "A woman needs a man like a fish needs a bicycle" was attributed to Gloria Steinem by *Time* magazine in autumn of 2000.

A summary of the phrase's origin from *The Phrase Finder's* www.phrases.org.uk website follows: Gloria Steinem in a note to *Time* magazine graciously acknowledged Irina Dunn, a distinguished Australian educator, journalist and politician for coining the aforementioned phrase back in 1970 when she was a student at the University of Sydney. Irina Dunn modestly admitted to paraphrasing an unnamed philosopher who said, "Man needs God like a fish needs a bicycle." Dunn said, "I scribbled the phrase on the backs of two toilet doors, would you believe?" Dunn's modesty of the logistical concept was appropriately acknowledged, as "'A needs a B like a C needs a D' was a well-established format in the USA many years before 1970."

Nonsense replaces common sense when a superfluous phrase's ambiguous interpretation effects cultural philosophy. No offense to either Gloria Steinem or Irina Dunn, a subjective interpretation of the phrase ultimately falls upon people's underestimation of the self-evident and invisible elements in nature's creation like love and oxygen. After all, God says in Genesis 2.18: "It is *not good that man should be alone; I will make him a helper comparable to him.*" Please also remember Genesis 2.7: *And the Lord God formed man of the dust of the ground, and breathed into his nostrils the breath of life; and man became a living being.*

A man and woman have the compatibility to compliment each other. Additionally, a man and woman thankfully have the ability to glorify God. More appropriate analogies follow: "A woman needs a man like a fish needs a school," and likewise "A man needs God like a fish needs a pool." Bumper stickers are not included.

Proliferation of the human race has a self-evident Constitutional foundation. Organization after organization is persistently being sold the following bill-of-goods, "If it happens in nature, it's natural." Does the fact that homosexuality occurs in nature really make it natural?

"Natural" means—existing in or formed by nature, according to the *Random House Webster's Dictionary*. This definition is a commonly accepted dictionary definition. Misinterpreting the word "existing" assumes that an "observable presence" constitutes "existing" through charlatan grandstanding. To expound the meaning of "existing," it's impossible for a baby to form from the homosexual activity of two women. It's equally difficult for two homosexual men to form an infant. Self-evidently, homosexuality unnaturally occurs in nature.

Longevity of a same-sex relationship is limited to the pair's lifetime. *The Declaration of Independence* records: "Prudence, indeed, will dictate that Governments long established should not be changed for light and transient causes." Provident consideration provides for the future that is not inherent within two homosexual's lifespans, and it's literally "politically correct" to preserve liberty and the pursuit of happiness that are derived from the Laws of Nature and Nature's God. A lobbyist representing the "sexual orientation" package isn't featuring the pros and cons in the presentation concerning homosexuality's transient causes. It's human nature to sympathize or empathize with an abused homosexual victim. After all, the tolerance of sexual orientation initially appears to extend kindness to another human being.

Simply doing something different is the primary impetus to change for the sake of change. Currently a powerful buzzword in society, "change" is arbitrary and not provident. Without provident consideration, arbitrary legislation refuses to substantiate homosexual laws with the Constitution. However, the Constitution outlines edifying standards for change. Change for the better is real change, and Constitutional change for the better always embraces past success as a asset and not as a detriment.

Greed is the primary motive for the misappropriated emphasis to change. Underestimating the assault on our Constitutional culture generates proposed legislation that contradicts the Constitution. Homosexuality's opposing Constitutional legislation assumes "openness" as an alternative meaning for "freedom." The Constitution models the institution of freedom after God's grace. What follows is John Jay's exponentiation concerning the Constitution's gracious invitation for common acceptance from the *Federalist Papers*: "Admit, for so is the fact, that this plan is only recommended, not imposed, but let it be remembered that it is neither recommended by blind approbation, nor the blind reprobation; but to the sedate and candid consideration which the magnitude and importance of the subject demand, and which it certainly ought to receive. But as has been already remarked that it is more wished than expected that it may be so considered and examined." A person's contemplation of self-evident truths exemplifies freedom. Our Constitution's axiom is not meant to be usurped.

Oppositions to the foundation of our culture in the Constitution are quite often instigated through exemplifying foreign cultures. Foreign relations inadequately assess the need to compromise our culture and conform in order to compete in the world market. American citizens are well advised to attend an orientation for the country of destination when traveling abroad. Also, people visiting our Country for extended lengths of time need a structured orientation concerning our American culture. Constitutional and cultural orientations are a timely consideration in light of the world's opposing cultures.

Simultaneously, the deliberate underemphasis America's historical appreciation outrageously is another ignored factor in public education's woes. Education's presentation of illiberal lobbying to remove the words "under God" in "The Pledge of Allegiance" discourages patriotism and is evident with the generational indifference of the United States' 225th Anniversary in 2001 for example.

A primary school teacher once taught me, "Remembering the date wasn't as important as the reason that event occurred in history. Although, the date was on the test." Appreciation of America's provident history was cherished not too long ago. The Constitution's inspired reason encouraged patriotic celebration in the past for instance the 1976 United States Bicentennial.

Misunderstanding "freedom of will" has been an enticing issue since the beginning of time. When the word "freedom" is used, fantasy has crept in to alter what history has Constitutionally reinforced. As soon as, someone gets physically, mentally or emotionally hurt is the point at which freedom ends.

Constitutionally, empathy confirms freedom before someone else is hurt. The *Declaration of Independence* references the Creator's natural parameters. Within the borders of freedom, a person remains safe, doesn't hurt others and rejects destructive enticement. Trespassing into openness happens. A person's unconstitutional condition leaves the person vulnerable. It's likely that the person's departure from the path of freedom buries the harmful source of abuse.

Openness and false assumptions have historically resided outside of the borders of freedom. With hasty same-sex union legislation, judges and other politicians have usurped their authority derived from the governed and assumed the people are credulous. In more than thirty states, the people have reclaimed their authority through referendums.

People who invariably pursue acceptance of illiberal behavior assume that a free society tolerates abuse, so Americans don't identify the self-evident detriments of an open society. Practices of openness in many instances are declared illegal and in homosexual instances ought to be. Legislating an open society actually is unconstitutional in America.

Not everyone is going to accept freedom with restriction. It's evident with the controversy regarding homosexual rights usurping human rights. It's no mystery why people's perceptions are awry. It's not difficult to figure out that an open homosexual society is unable to sustain itself and does not promote the common good. Homosexuals have the same human rights as all people of any race, color, creed and national origin. But, homosexuality's legislation to extinction disregards the borders of human rights.

Homosexual groups have relentlessly lobbied politicians, so they have attempted to compromise freedom to include their unnatural behavior under the sun. The Laws of Nature and Nature's God have defined the self-evidence of a pursuit in Ecclesiastes 1.9 and follow, "That which has been is what will be, that which is done is what will be done, and there is nothing new under the sun." Homosexually tolerant rulers have coerced histories with no happy endings because specious assumptions of prejudiced have ignored and misconstrued human preservation. Moreover, the Founding Fathers admonished us to pursue happiness on the prudent course that is recorded in the *Declaration of Independence*.

Our Country's citizens are comprised primarily from descendants of immigrants who pursued freedom. Common defense, human rights and provident consideration have been some of the axiomatic freedoms that we have cherished. In our will to survive, common values have continued to bind us together. Our heroes have earned respect because they are people who have fought and have continued to preserve freedom.

In the long run, we're not doing homosexuality any public service with the acceptance of tolerance because tolerance currently corrupts the people's meaning of the common welfare. *The Declaration of Independence* expounds the following: "That mankind are more disposed to suffer, while evils are sufferable, than to right themselves by abolishing the forms to which they are accustomed. But when a long train of abuses and usurpations, pursuing invariably the same Object evinces a design to reduce them under a absolute Despotism, it is their right, it is their duty, to throw off such Government, and to provide new Guards for their future security." Our declared rights allow us to legislate that same-sex relationships are an intolerable cause because homosexuality's transient cause threatens the very existence of all humankind.

In consideration of a person's formulation of an opinion, it's apparent that a person's safety zone or comfort level influences one's own opinion. If a person's home has an electronic security system, deadbolt locks and shatterproof glass, the person has a great sense of safety. The other more common home security system is a locked door. Moreover, a person of faith embraces God's home security system as recorded in Proverbs 3.33: *He* (God) *blesses the home of the just.* Security is not new. Throughout history, a fort-like wall with a mote has encompassed many military compounds and communities.

A false sense of security appears to be the assumption of many illiberal opinion columns and commentaries. Frequently, an author wants to support preemptive legislation, but the opinion falls on deaf ears. This instance occurs when the person in a position of power isn't an advocate for the common good. Self-assertion that violates the populous' common welfare is not much more than selfishness. When the common good isn't even an after thought to support a selfish opinion, this type of duress rarely receives the community's support. A dictator is rarely able to admit a wrong decision in order to be a "bigger person" and accept self-evident truths.

Regretfully, the mass media has the ability to destructively propagate public opinion. The statement, "A computer saves money" is one such assumption. "Does a computer honestly save money?" Unstable technology opposes accountability as expounded in Chapter Six. The revolution of the computer culture is capricious making us less civilized. One step forward is the epitome of the advancement in computer software technology with the denial of two steps back. A consumer pays the price for software advancement because software unaccountably functions hence constant updates. It is unconscionable that such instability is commonly accepted as accountable. What is happening?

Now, we are like a family of immigrants living in computer-land. Parents are already overwhelmed with the additional requirement to conform to the unstable computer subculture. Children entering school face the challenge of tolerating computer jargon. Then, children return home from school to educate parents. Instead of parent's values being the primary influence for children, children are the propagators of the pervading computer subculture. Desires of children to inherit the values of our ancestors are under-emphasized because of the overwhelming mandate to compromise for the sake of technology. Progressive and comprehensive advances in the public education curricula are the euphemism for demoralized, ineffective public education.

With the entertainment subculture's inundating proposition: "Do not confront homosexuals," the entertainment subculture has transmuted the general population's perception from natural priorities. Mom at one time traditionally was first in our hearts. Her homemade pie was third. Baseball of course was second. The phrase that is no longer appreciated is, "Mom, baseball and apple pie." The entertainment subculture currently emphasizes the American society's priorities as "homosexuality, computers and fast-food."

Most of us admit that our Country has become quite different than 234 years ago. We are all immigrants into a radical state of existence that most of us didn't imagine would be so convoluted.

It's been a sufferable course to admit that homosexuality hasn't been placed under proper scrutiny. The name-calling when someone questions homosexuality has nearly always been retaliated with the presumption of prejudice. From the *Federalist Papers,* James Madison wrote: "By faction, I understand a number of citizens whether amounting to a majority or a minority of the whole, who are united or actuated by some common impulse of passion, or of interest, adverse to the rights of other citizens, or to the permanent or aggregate interests of the community. There are two methods to curing the mischiefs of faction: the one by removing its causes; the other, by controlling the effects." James Madison had authored those words because the *US Constitution* had been criticized and labeled "treasonous" from sympathizers of Great Britain's despotism.

In continuing with human nature, any attempt to further victimize the human race needs to simply be combated with the declaration, "homosexuality is unnatural." This truth is a liberating phrase. *The US Constitution* exemplifies the common good with the words "We the people." A decent respect of the opinions of humankind abandons transient aspirations acknowledging selflessness instead of selfishness.

Victims

Our Country's history holds the key to survival. As old as the hills, people are celebrating through voting, writing and communicating with their political representatives exercising free speech. To recover from the disaster propagated through the homosexual lobbying, immoral education and computer revolution, it is necessary to reclaim the rights that we have allowed to diminish while praying for our political representatives. The way that we are celebrating our Constitutional freedom is adopting a cause that we preserve the freedom in which our ancestors sought and many times fought to acquire. The fact that freedom is still a concept is amazing; since, bureaucracy attempts to eliminate freedom. The person who refuses to accept bureaucratic legislation is a hero.

If public education genuinely wants to contribute to our society then preserve traditional terminology. Progress in education should mean a change for the better and not the opposing trend. For example, self respect shouldn't hinge on primary school children discovering their sexual orientation. Public education still ought to emphasize innocuously treating others the same way that a person would like to be treated. If true dignity was an emphasis in the curriculum, bullying or cyberbullying would decrease.

In considering the heart of public education's departure from traditional morals, public education's perplexity follows: "Who's to say what good morals are?" How about if morals in education reflects our Country's Constitution? However, as expounded in Chapter Five, morals education is being redefined to include sexual orientation. Because public education prefers not to fully disclose the sexual education curriculum, redefinition of morals needs to be exposed. Proverbs 4.23 implores; *Keep your heart with all diligence, for out of it spring the issues of life.* In this case, the heart of the issue is the Constitution. Unless Constitutional education is legislated and monitored, immoral education continues to be unaccountable with multiple diversions and "Band Aid" issues.

Incidents of bullying and cyberbullying students are escalating in public education. Concurrently, traditional morals are being substituted with the sexual orientation philosophy in the curricula. Reactions to bullying instead of being proactive are counterproductive.

Misappropriation of the bullying issue in public education is like the whining of a child with a maladjusted attitude. Tolerance of an inadequately educated child's attitude ignores homosexuality's double-standard. An abusive homosexual degrades a victim with the same bullying that the assailant declares as "prejudiced." The fact is that the escalation of bullying is a symptom of education's demoralized curriculum. Public education is in denial. A person doesn't have to think too long to realize a volatile attitude needs adjustment. Can a spoiled child restore morals in public education?

Prioritizing good morals education needs attention. The existence of complacent attitudes begins with the idea that delinquency is tolerable as long as it doesn't obviously affect people. This precipitous attitude blinds people. A smokescreen is evident to redirect people's focus away from the importance of morals in education. It is certain that the exponents of the bullying issue have deliberately instigated its ineffectual diversion as the preoccupation of the Twenty-first Century.

A roadblock on the path to learning is so-called "homosexual tolerance." An axiomatic example of the learning process examines the progression of learning mathematics in Chapter Five. Recalling a person's own comprehensive learning experience is sufficient to axiomatically recognize how a person learns.

The challenge of learning that requires a student to tolerate homosexuality obstructs a person's learning potential. Although public education is the primary point of concern, prudence is a subject of contention in the Evangelical Lutheran Church Association (ELCA). The ELCA condones pastors in committed homosexual relationships through its synod vote effective in August of 2009. The roadblock condoning homosexuality causes division instigating individuals as well as entire congregations to separate from the church under duress.

Similarly, exodus of students from public education occurs because sexual education requires tolerance of homosexuality. Education administrator's dictatorial attitude from a variety of learning institutions demands compliance. Whether in education or a religion's instruction, condoning sexual orientation's tolerance is void of Constitutional consideration. Although a sexual education educator may sporadically reference the Constitution as a foundation for tolerance, homosexuality's transient cause is tolerated in sexual education.

The people's discontent reveals a referendum as the only means to counteract arbitrary judicial legislation. Overturning same-sex partnership legislation has occurred in thirty-plus states through the people's referendum process. During the time of the writing, the Western US District Court is hearing a case attempting to repeal California's Proposition 8 affirmative referendum. Since its November 2008 approval, Proposition 8 bans gay marriage overturning a prior California judicial decision approving gay marriage.

According to the January 11, 2010, *Associated Press* release by Lisa Leff, "Walker's court is the first to employ live witnesses in the task....academic experts from the fields of political science, history, psychology and economics."

The provident consideration alarm is sounding. Public education currently immerses itself in homosexuality's inhumane view that is absent of provident consideration. The education subculture is the same group that utters "moral" but tolerates "immorality."

The following information was compiled from *Courthouse News Service's* www.courthousenews.com website, "Advocacy Groups Lose Prop 8 Records Appeal" by Elizabeth Banicki published April 14, 2010: The court comprised of three judges from California's US District rejected homosexuality's appeal of Proposition 8 campaign materials. The plaintiff's Proposition 8 campaign materials were court-ordered for full disclosure, but the groups representing the plaintiff refused to release the materials to the defense. Same-sex marriage's advocates attempted to appeal the court's request to turnover the documents, however at the time of this writing, the judges didn't honor the appeal because the homosexual groups were not yet held in contempt for withholding the pertinent materials.

If homosexuality's repeal of Proposition 8 in US District Court succeeds, then, an unconstitutional premise potentially prohibits the referendum process from banning gay marriage. Homosexuality's pursuit of judicial legislation precariously attempts to remove the Constitutional right for citizens to propose a referendum, confirm the Constitution and restore freedom. Enforcing a monarchy usurps our Government by the people and for the people. Regardless of the outcome, an appeal of the ruling is more than likely eminent for the US Supreme Court.

An unconstitutional ruling impedes the people's right to a referendum. Please contemplate the following excerpt from *The Washington Post's* www.washingtonpost.com website, "D.C. Judge rules against marriage referendum"by Tim Craig published January 15, 2010: "D.C. Superior Court judge ruled Thursday that same-sex marriage opponents do not have a right to call for a referendum to determine whether such unions should be legal in the District." In addition, the District of Columbia is unconstitutionally lobbying US Congress' approval for statehood.

You may very well be reading this when the US Supreme Court hears an appeal of California's Proposition 8. Although with the people's referendum and the US Supreme Courts' adherence to the Constitution, an appeal on behalf of the citizens in the District of Columbia ought to be on the agenda.

All true communication is from God. If we want to help someone with God's love, would you say that helping someone is politically correct? 1 John 4.8 *God is love.* An illogical homosexual argument for lust follows: If God is love, and all love is from God; then, why can't two homosexuals that love each other be married? True love does not harm a neighbor as Romans 13.9-10 confirm: *You shall love your neighbor as yourself. Love does no harm to a neighbor; therefore, love is the fulfillment of the law.* So-called "homosexual love" is not God's love. Although, homosexual lust abuses and humiliates with unnatural and vile passions.

It is a detrimental trait from the Word of God for homosexuals to speak empty words: Ephesians 5.6: *Let no one deceive you with empty words.* Just because a homosexual says that homosexuality is love, subjectivity does not make it a fact. In fact, it is nearly impossible for homosexuals to know God. Romans 1.32: *Who, knowing the righteous judgment of God, that those who practice such things are deserving of death, not only do the same but also approve of those who practice them.* For the person whom deliberately chooses self-destruction the wages of sin are death through contradicting or denying God. However in Psalms 107.20, the Bible reveals God's mercy to repentant souls and follows: *He sent His word and healed them, and delivered them from their own destruction.*

In the King James Version (KJV), the Greek word *arsenokoitēs* is translated *defile themselves with mankind* and *abusers of themselves with mankind* in 1 Timothy 1.10 and 1 Corinthians 6.9, respectively. In the NKJV, both entries of the word *arsenokoitēs* are simply translated *sodomites. Arsenokoitēs* is represented as an attempt to usurp coitus which is the natural reproductive relationship between a man and woman.

Both of the words translated "men" in the phrase "men with men" are the Greek word *arsen.* Romans 1.27: *Likewise also the men, leaving the natural use of the woman, burned in their lust one for another, men with men committing what is shameful, and receiving in themselves the penalty of their error which was due.* The reproductive and nutritive contributions that are characteristics of a man with a woman are inherent in the Greek word *arsen.* Therefore, men with men are committing that which is shameful Natural marriage relationships represent the contributions of a man and woman with the word "coitus."

A closely related word to the Greek word *arsen* in the English language is "arson." According to the *Random House Webster's Dictionary,* arson means: the malicious burning of property, and coitus means: sexual intercourse, esp. between a man and woman. Clearly according to God, a homosexual relationship is sexual abuse abandoning the complementary contributions of a male and female. Expansively, *arsenokoitēs* means: unnatural and harmful sexual abuse inflicted on a person of the same sex that attempts to sentence the victim to eternal destruction by fire.

Homosexuality is unnatural. If toxic waste is poured in water, this unnatural abuse of a natural resource makes it nearly impossible to remove the poison. A water treatment plant may strain, filter and heat water to purify it. Similarly, homosexuality inflicts havoc in a human being with the physical and mental complications. It affects speech, movement and feelings. However when a human being is homosexually abused, God is able deliver the person from the power of darkness.

Miraculously in the name of Jesus Christ, a homosexual may be cleansed from all unrighteousness by confession of sins to God. 1 John 1.9: *If we confess our sins, He is faithful and just to forgive us our sins and to cleanse us from all unrighteousness.* Unlike a water filtration plant, God cleanses us from all unrighteousness. No pollution remains. However, please remember God's faithfulness. That's why in 1 John 1.9 God's Word says that God is faithful. A reformed homosexual is forgiven but needs to remember that God is faithful and just to forgive us our sins and to cleanse us from all unrighteousness. Romans 12.2: *And do not be conformed to this world, but be transformed by the renewing of your mind, that you may prove what is that good and acceptable and perfect will of God.* Meditation on the scripture from the perspective of the Word of God gives believers depth to their relationship with God. To be conformed to this world is not to accept God's faithfulness to forgive.

Homosexual victims' recoveries are often life-long lessons reconciling that they were victims of hate. Homosexual abuses are hate crimes. All homosexuals have been sexually abused. Improper use, not following the instructions and simply disregarding what God meant for a relationship between a married man and woman have caused no small amount of confusion distinguishing between love and hate. Proverbs 1.29-30: *Because they hated knowledge and did not choose the fear of the Lord. They would have none of my counsel* and *despised my every rebuke.* In addition, all homosexuals are verbally abused and threatened. Unconscionably, homosexual victims are humiliated with a threat similar to the following: "You'll suffer harm if you tell anyone what has been done to you." Threats instigate that there is no real love indicative of the absence of unreported homosexual abuse. Vile passions inherently are abusive in homosexuality's destructive nature.

For Christians, common goals encompass enriching traditional marriage with God at the center. For a non-Christian marriage, common goals are not always as clearly defined with the absence of God at the center of their relationship. Emotional, financial and physical responsibilities require participation and compromise from both a man and a woman in a natural marriage. A man and woman equally need to admit that the other partner is far better equipped to fulfill the spouse's portion of a marital responsibility.

The life-long commitment with a mate requires God's blessing. Lustful gratification requires no commitment. "Vile affection" doesn't define a "committed relationship." God promises a companion for each person. God's affirmation follows in 1 Corinthians 7.2: *Nevertheless, because of sexual immorality, let each man have his own wife, and let each woman have her own husband.* "The family that prays together stays together."

Chapter 9
Deliverance From Evil on Three Strategic Fronts

Constitutional wisdom tells us that "Constitutional Correctness" is the Christian standard of "political correctness" and more often than not agrees with a our religion's views. The Constitution's centrist position provides a political reference for the common good of all people.

The following biblical parody recollects Solomon's wisdom considering some of our Nation's judicial challenges:

Sol emerged from the judge's chamber clothed in the traditional, floor-length, black rob. He marched reverently to his seat wisely carrying a Bible in respect of his judicial responsibility. As it was when the people were unable to resolve their differences, he granted them audience to decide which person innocently pursued happiness.

Hannah and Jessa appeared with a child before Sol, the judge. They each held one of the child's hands, and they both exhibited some anxiety. The three stood in the judge's presence waiting to be acknowledged to speak.

Sol said, "Young lady, please state your dispute" motioning to Jessa to speak first. He added, "Proceed!"

Jessa said, " Your honor, I humbly request that this child may continue to be taught in school that a same-sex relationship is a good choice. A homosexual relationship can care for a child just as good as a heterosexual couple."

Sol waited to ensure that Jessa had spoke her peace and responded, "Very well!" Then, he swiveled his chair slightly to acknowledge Hannah and said, "Young lady, what have you to say concerning this child?"

Hannah said, "Your honor, I humbly request the court's mercy, so the child may be taught the importance of a natural marriage relationship in school. The child tells me that she's learning that choosing homosexuality is good, but I would like the child to have the opportunity someday to know the joy of being a parent."

With the participants in the dispute having stated their cases, Sol looked into their eyes which seemed like an eternity. Then Sol motioned to the bailiff and declared, "Execute the child!"

Silence filled the courtroom. Jessa uttered not a word waiting for enforcement of the judge's ruling to execute the child. While Hannah gasped and with tears cried-out, "Your Honor, please let Jessa educate the child. I withdraw my dispute."

Some people cheered in the courtroom, and others wept as the bailiff led the child from the courtroom.

Then, Judge Sol pounded his gavel and commanded, "Order in the court. Bailiff, release the child into Hannah's custody because Hannah values the child's life over death. While, Jessa was willing to sacrifice both the child's perception and life. Jessa has confirmed with her indifference that she has no sincere concern for the child's well-being. Homosexuality may no longer be taught in school as a good relationship because it's an unnatural teaching to a child's detriment"

Later, the bailiff approached the judge and said, "You're the only judge in the land that ruled in favor on this issue; such a ruling is considered prejudiced. Who are these people; why did you overturn your decision?" Judge Sol said, "When I made my final ruling, I had to make the ruling as though the existence of the human race depended on the child. If the child grew-up and chose an unnatural relationship, the child would be unable to have children. Therefore, Hannah's innocent intention confirmed that she was the child's mother. While, Jessa's disdain exposed homosexuality's volatile nature."

One of the most misunderstood concepts is judgment. To capitalize on judgment's lack of clarity, homosexuality misuses the Bible in its defense. John 8.7 is one such verse: *He who is without sin among you, let him throw a stone at her first.* God clarifies His judgment in Romans *2.1: Therefore you are inexcusable, O man, whoever you are who judge, for in whatever you judge another you condemn yourself; for you who judge practice the same things.* If a person is a practicing homosexual, the person has no right to throw a stone or judge for or against homosexuality. God defines a conflict of interest. Yes, the judicial ethic of a biased self benefit is quite often grounds to excuse a judge from a case. For example, it's not an ethical practice for a judge who practices unnatural homosexuality to legislate homosexuality from the bench.

Homosexuality's openness is not synonymous with freedom in America. Constitutional freedom does not violate the Laws of Nature and Nature's God; while, homosexuality's openness does. However, the attempted assault on the two angels reveals that homosexuality's openness was politically accepted in Sodom and Gomorrah in Genesis 19.4: *Now before they lay down, the men of the city, the men of Sodom, both old and young, all the people from every quarter, surrounded the house.*

The attempted homosexual assault escalated in Genesis 19.6-9: *So Lot went out to them through the doorway, shut the door behind him, and said, "Please, my brethren, do not do so wickedly! See now, I have two daughters who have not known a man; please, let me bring them out to you, and you may do to them as you wish; only do nothing to these men, since this is the reason they have come under the shadow of my roof." And they said, "Stand back!" Then they said, "This one came to stay here, and he keeps acting as a judge; now we will deal worse with you than with them." So they pressed hard against the man Lot, and came near to break down the door.* Homosexuality's political correctness refused to recognize Lot's authority or judgment to protect the men (angels) in Sodom and Gomorrah.

Notice that Lot didn't deny God's judgment. Nor did he explain that he agreed with God. Without reason, a homosexual abuser that is hellbent on continuing to abuse rarely can be purged from the premeditated course of lust. However with God's wisdom, Lot attempted to divert the homosexuals' lust. It was Lot's self sacrifice to offer his two daughters; however as a parent, he did not want anyone harmed especially his family. God forbid that a soul should be confronted with a homosexual assault.

Thankfully, the Constitution provides the foundation for us to legislate laws against homosexual abuse. In continuing to review Genesis 19, blindness impairs the homosexuals' instigation to abuse, and Lot escapes.

For people whom deliberately oppose and refuse to accept God, they often walk too far beyond the boundaries of God's universal protection (the rain that falls on the just and unjust). For instance, homosexual lobbyists oppose the Laws of Nature and Nature's God and disregard the parameters of freedom.

Manifesting God's respectful distance between you and an abuser occurs in His presence. The respectful distance or "GAP" acronym follows:

Go to God for Guidance.
Assert the Applicable Alternative.
Pray for Proper Protection.

Allocate time in your daily schedule to pray for protection. God isn't forsaking you. Personal time with God starts a person off on the right foot to determine the day's activities. If you're already running late with a busy schedule, essential prayer is equally as important as wearing a pair of shoes. Praying for enough time to pray is also a noble request.

When a person faces an ungodly adversary, worldly wisdom doesn't assist in deliverance. A respectful distance from the "GAP" acronym relies solely on God's guidance. Conviction that God is you and with you is more important than physical strength. Although, God may direct you in physical defense. Because of the countless scenarios, God always has an answer for you. When God directs you to implement an action that does not agree with worldly wisdom, it needs to be done. For that matter, worldly wisdom has nothing to do with the *US Constitution*.

Have you ever looked into the eyes of evil? When you do, the image is not easily forgotten. I was thirteen years-old. After visiting with a friend, I called for a ride. But, my Father wasn't home. I told my Mother that I'd walk to the nearby business district then call again to see if he was home.

As I walked to the business district, I saw what I thought to be my Dad's car. So I ran, opened the car's door and hopped-in. To my dismay, it was not my Dad in the car. The surly man gloated at me and said, "That was easy." My attempt to open the door was to no avail. The car door's master-lock was in the hands of the predator.

The presumptuous captor sordidly attempted to stun me. But, God's peace was with me. Without wavering, God gave me words of knowledge that convinced the the attempted abductor to release the master-lock. So, I was able to open the door to the car. I was on my way home. Thankful for a miracle, I praised God every step of the way. I acknowledged God and applied the principles from "GAP." Additionally, God told me that I would see the degenerate man sometime in the future.

Many years later, I called the National Center for Missing and Exploited Children (NCMEC) because I saw my attempted abductor. Not to report my attempted abduction but I reported what had come to my attention from a a more

Victims

recent abduction. Of course, what God told me was not what NCMEC wanted to hear. To my knowledge, the child molester has not been apprehended.

Prayer that promises peace also gives a believer confidence to overcome other subtle verbal attacks. An unbeliever is unable to comprehend God's peace. A Christian anticipates some of the following responses to startling inconsideration: Are you living under a rock? No! Is the Bible like cast in stone? Yes! Just because everyone else accepts the Bible as literal, does that mean you have to accept it? If I may inquire, by "everyone," are you referring to the children of the Most High? Instigation of an endless collection of lies is a premeditated attack to stun a child of God. Thick skin has nothing to do with coping with criticism, but walking with the Spirit does elevate a believer above nonsense.

We need to obtain understanding for complete deliverance from the moment we get born again, during our walk with God on earth and eternally. 2 Corinthians 1.10 reads: *Who delivered us from so great a death, and does deliver us; in whom we trust He will yet deliver* us. When the images of deliverance are foggy, we fall short of enriching our walk with God. We are complete in our body, soul and spirit when we are born again. We walk in the light as He is the light with His Word as our guide. With God's fellowship in mind, we ask for forgiveness to maintain our Father-child relationships.

Your time with God and His son Jesus Christ will be completely joyful for all eternity. Thinking of the most memorable time that you have ever spent with your earthly family will give you a little bit of an idea what our eternal family will be like. God provides vital examples for you to draw from like the loving family relationship in 2 Corinthians 6.18: *"I will be a Father to you, and you shall be My sons and daughters," says the Lord Almighty.*

A believer will have eternal individuality which encourages self respect while patiently waiting for Christ's return. 1 Corinthians 15.35: *But someone will say, "How are the dead raised up? And with what body do they come?"* You will notice that our bodies will be changed if we are asleep or alive at the time of Christ's return in 1 Corinthians 15.51: *Behold I show you a mystery: We shall not all sleep, but shall all be changed.* From the theme of Paul's letter, God will inspire each of us with His unique respect for each believer's new body. 1 Corinthians 15.37-38: *And what you sow, you do not sow that body that shall be, but mere grain—perhaps wheat or some other grain. But God gives it a body as He pleases, and to each seed its own body.* God likens a passed away believer in the grave as a seed. A farmer or gardener will plant quality seed that turns into a quality plant and bears quality fruit. According to God at

Christ's coming, a believer will maintain individuality as He said: *But God gives it a body as He pleases, and to each seed its own body.* Your new body will have incorruptibility beyond what you're currently capable to comprehend.

Adam and Eve were initially clothed with God's life; until, they esteemed the knowledge of good and evil over life. After their transgression, the knowledge of good and evil caused them to fear. They were on the road to death. They sewed fig leaves together to cover themselves. They hid themselves among the trees of the garden from God because they were naked.

God's love is such that He plans that we will be clothed with life as recorded in 2 Corinthians 5.4: *For we who are in* this *tent groan, being burdened, not because we want to be unclothed, but further clothed, that mortality may be swallowed up by life.* We presently have the armor of God; until, we are fully clothed.

When abused victims surrender their defense mechanisms, their minds are altered, and their minds surrender—basically give-up. In many cases of homosexual abuse, victims of homosexual physical and mental abuse totally suppress any memory of the abuse and the abuser. The minds of homosexuals are described in Romans 1.28: *And even as they did not like to retain God in* their *knowledge, God gave them over to a debased mind, to do those things that are not fitting.* Homosexuals with debased minds are defiant of God's order of things even natural laws like gravity. Many biblical examples exist including our Lord's temptation to throw himself from the pinnacle of the temple. Jesus replied in Matthew 4.7: *"You shall not tempt the Lord your God."* Jesus' victories establish hope for people whom are stripped of their mental defenses through abuse. Jesus' assertions in Matthew chapter four overcoming temptation are applicable today. With confession of Jesus as Lord, then, we are His creation.

God never meant for anyone to be deceived. Hebrews 3.13-14: *But exhort one another daily, while it is called "today," lest anyone of you be hardened through the deceitfulness of sin. For we have become partakers of Christ if we hold the beginning of our confidence steadfast to the end.* A believer had a humble beginning as a new creation. The favorite verse of scripture that you cherish or the song in your heart had eternal potential right from the start.

Homosexuality has been around for a long time. In the United States, the theory of "accepting people for whom they are" is loosely based on the *US Constitution*. However, the Constitutional premise includes freedom for people of different race, color, creed and national origin but not destructive choice. An infant does not have input concerning the baby's language, skin color, religion and birthplace that are inherent characteristics from the child's parents. A destructive lifestyle like homosexuality has been incorrectly elevated to the level a culture. Currently, an adoptive parent's innocuous pursuit of happiness for a child is compromised considering the homosexual subculture's inappropriate elevation as a basis for adoption.

Homosexual abuse is a crime of hate. The choice to commit a criminal act of homosexual abuse is a crime and ought to be persecuted in a court of law. The Laws of Nature and Nature's God excludes homosexuality from Constitutional legislation. Jude 1:7 *As Sodom and Gomorrah, and the cities around them in a similar manner to these, having given themselves over to sexual immortality and gone after strange flesh, are set forth as an example, suffering the vengeance of eternal fire.* Eternal fire is the choice of unrepentant homosexuals. Alternatively, the benefit of choosing God's Word is recorded in Proverbs 2.4-5: *If you seek her as silver, and search for her as for hidden treasures; Then you will understand the fear of the Lord and find the knowledge of God.*

The opposite of homosexual behavior includes repentance. It is our privilege as believers to enjoy fellowship with our Heavenly Father through His son Jesus Christ. John 14.6: *Jesus said to him, I am the way, the truth, and the life. No one comes to the Father except through Me.* Honestly assess the value of God in your life. Be thankful for all of the blessings that He has bestowed upon and around you.

Cherish the truth through prayer, guarding your heart and mind. Your heart's desire is God's privilege to provide you. Ephesians 5:1-2: *Therefore be imitators of God as dear children. And walk in love, as Christ also has loved us and given himself for us, an offering and a sacrifice to God for a sweet smelling aroma.*

I am so thankful to God for the Christian ministries that contribute to preserve human rights. 1 Corinthians 12.5-6: *There are differences of ministries but the same Lord. And there are diversities of activities, but it is the same God that works all in all.* Likewise, I am so thankful to God for the individuals who stand against the power of darkness. 1 Corinthians 12.11-12: *But one and the same Spirit works all these things, distributing to each one individually as He wills. For as the body is one and has many members, but all the members of that one body, being many, are one body, so also is Christ.* Without Christianity's adherence, Jesus' prophesy would be different, but in Matthew 24.37-38, He said, *"But as the days of Noah were, so also will the coming of the Son of Man be. For as in the days before the flood, they were eating and drinking, marrying and giving in marriage, until the day that Noah entered the ark."* Your labor in the Lord is not in vain. Marriage is preserved according to God.

The drug, education and mass media subcultures are inappropriately convinced that the homosexual subculture financially benefits their interests. Therefore, all of those subculture's philosophies are pervaded with homosexual abusers' disregard for divine providence. When the primary operating philosophy revolves around homosexuality, the dynamics of the subcultures depend on complying to so-called "diversity." Instead of four destructive subcultures, they are destructively one in purpose. Even with the homosexual subculture's infiltration of the medical subculture supplanting "homosexuality" from the list of mental diseases, the Constitutional Laws of Nature and Nature's God remain the authoritative standard. However, the educational, political and religious subcultures are the three strategic fronts that require attention so that the subcultures adhere to the Laws of Nature and Nature's God.

A government institution like the US Department of Education or political representation has a Constitutional responsibility to operate within the parameters of the *US Constitution*. Constitutional diversity includes the human cultures of race, color, creed or national origin and not a homosexual subculture. It's imperative that our political stance resides on Constitutional ground and does not tolerate any political institution's compromise to our *US Constitution*.

Yes, the Constitution's axiomatic laws are inspired by God who is the Creator. We must not allow diversions from the task at hand.

Homosexuality's diversions like accusing Christians of apostatizing instigate discrimination against the Constitution's human cultures and are unacceptable. Our political challenges reside in rescinding preemptive legislation and not tolerating legislation founded on unsubstantiated transparency which is based on conjecture.

Constitutional and natural considerations result in "a decent respect of the opinions of mankind" which is written in the *Declaration of Independence*. Decent and respectful opinions declare that unnatural political acts of legislation are unconstitutional because unnatural acts of legislation are detrimental for our entire culture. Homosexuality's legislative motives instigating unsubstantiated openness are not synonymous with nature's self-evidence. In America, people are open to express their opinions, but Constitutional rights do not extend freedom to legislate unnatural opinions. We have God's hand of blessing in the United States' Documents of Freedom. We are not boastful of our victory, and we remain thankful to God through Jesus Christ our Lord.

The United States of America isn't changing its name to "Sodom and Gomorrah." The "pursuit of happiness" doesn't imply that destructive pursuits result in happiness. In truth, the *Declaration of Independence's* self-evidence expounds that unnatural behavior ends with an unnatural result.

Jesus expounded the consequences of Sodom and Gomorrah's political sin in six New Testament citations. Jesus illustrated self-evidence when he said in Matthew 7.19-20, *"Ever tree that does not bear good fruit is cut down and thrown into the fire. Therefore by their fruits you will know them."* Respect for the Laws of Nature and Nature's God during the cultivation process determined if the seed was fruitful. America has honored self-evidence as the authority for legislation for nearly 234 years.

Please allow time in your busy life to appreciate your integral importance to encourage legislation from the Creator's perspective. A discreet reminder to the educational, religious and political subcultures helps to cultivate adherence to our Documents of Freedom. Acknowledging God, our victory resides in legislative advocacy. Proverbs 29.26 reads: *Many seek the ruler's favor, but justice for man* comes *from the Lord.* To God be the glory.

Proverbs: People's Perception of Priorities
Reference and Scripture

Proverbs 18.20-21: *A man's stomach shall be satisfied from the fruit of his mouth;* from the produce of his mouth he shall be filled. *Death and life are in the power of the tongue and they that love it shall eat its fruit.*

Proverbs 3.18: *She* (God's wisdom and understanding) is *a tree of life to those who take hold of her, and happy* are all *who retain her.*

Proverbs 1.7: *The fear* (acknowledgment of God's respectful omnipotence) *of the Lord is the beginning of knowledge.*

Proverbs 3.5-6: *Trust is the Lord with all your heart, and lean not unto your own understanding. In all your ways acknowledge Him, and He shall direct your paths.*

Proverbs 4.7: *Wisdom is the principal thing; therefore get wisdom. And in all your getting, get understanding.*

Proverbs 2.8-12: *He guards the paths of justice, and preserves the way of His saints. Then you will understand righteousness, justice, and equity and every good path. When wisdom enters your heart, and knowledge is pleasant to your soul, discretion will preserve you; understanding will keep you, to deliver you from evil, from the man who speaks perverse things.*

Proverbs 30.18-19 (KJV): *There are three* things which *are too wonderful for me, yea, four which I know not. The way of an eagle in the air, the way of a serpent upon a rock, the way of a ship in the midst of the sea, and the way of a man with a maid.*

Proverbs 25.11: *A word fitly spoken* is like *apples of gold in settings of silver.*

Proverbs 3.33: *He (God) blesses the home of the just.*

Proverbs 4.23: *Keep your heart with all diligence, for out of it springs the issues of life.*

Proverbs 1.29-30: *Because they hated knowledge and did not choose the fear of the Lord. They would have none of my counsel and despised my every rebuke.*

Proverbs 2.4-5: *If you seek her as silver, and search for her as for hidden treasures; Then you will understand the fear of the Lord and find the knowledge of God.*

Proverbs 29.26: *Many seek the ruler's favor, but justice for man from the Lord.*

A collection of Proverbs from this writing for your enjoyment.

Notes

CHAPTER ONE: Preaching the Forbidden Fruit to the Choir
Hamilton, Brady E., PhD; Martin, Joyce A., MPH; and Ventura, Stephanie J., MA, Division of Vital Statistics. "Births: Preliminary Data for 2007, National Vital Statistics Reports."Nation Center for Health Statistics (NCHS), Center for Disease Control and Prevention's (CDC), Washington, D.C., Online, http://www.cdc.gov/nchs/data/nvsr/nvsr57/nvsr57_12.pdf.

CHAPTER THREE: The Origin Indicates the Outcome
Olfson, Mark MD, MPH; Steven C. Marcus, PhD. "National Patterns in Antidepressant Medication Treatment." Arch Gen Psychiatry, Chicago, Illinois, 2009;66(8):848-856. Online, http://archpsyc.ama-assn.org/cgi/content/abstract/66/8/848.

Keyword: No Child Left Behind Act of 2001, sexual orientation, "No Child Left Behind Act of 2001, Equal Access to Public School Facilities, Definitions and Rule." US Government Printing Office, Washington, D.C., p. 1067.
http://www.gpo.gov/fdsys/pkg/CRPT-107hrpt334/pdf/CRPT-107hrpt334.pdf.

Keyword: No Child Left Behind Act of 2001, sexual orientation, "US Department of Education Strategic Plan, 2002-2007, Department of Education Mission." US Department of Education, Washington, D.C., p.2.
http://find.ed.gov/search?client=default_frontend&output=xml_no_dtd&proxystylesheet=default_frontend&q=US+Department+of+Education+Strategic+Plan%2C+2002-2007&sa.x=18&sa.y=5

Keyword: 2010, Department of Education's Mission, "The Department of Education, Office of Inspector General." US Department of Education, Washington, D.C., p.1.
http://www2.ed.gov/about/offices/list/oig/auditreports/fy2010/l03k0002.pdf

Keyword: John Wesley. Wikopedia The Free Encyclopedia, San Francisco, California, Online, http://en.wikipedia.org/wiki/John_Wesley.

Keyword: Sexual violence,
"Statewide plan to prevent sexual violence to be launched Friday."
Minnesota Department of Health,
St. Paul, Minnesota, June 5, 2008, Online,
www.health.state.mn.us/news/pressrel/svp060508.html.

Keyword: Public policy entities,
"Messaging Action Team."
Minnesota Department of Health,
St. Paul, Minnesota, September 15, 2009, Online,
www.health.state.mn.us/svp/documents/messaging.pdf.

Keyword: Abstinence, "House Research Bill." Minnesota State Legislature, St. Paul, Minnesota, Online, http://www.house.leg.state.mn.us/hrd/bs/83/HF0580.html.

CHAPTER FOUR: The Outcome Indicates the Origin
Hamilton, Alexander. The Federalist Papers. Chutchogue, New York, Buccaneer Book, Inc., 1992, p. 3.

Keyword: Hate Crimes Prevention Act, "Matthew Shepard Act and James Byrd Jr. Hate Crimes Prevention Act." US Government Printing Office, Washington, D.C., Sec. 4701-13, Online,
http://www.gpo.gov/fdsys/pkg/PLAW-111publ84/pdf/PLAW-111publ84.pdf

Keyword: Mike Pence, Republican Indiana, antithetical. "PENCE CALLS HATE CRIMES PROVISION IN DEFENSE BILL 'UNCONSCIONABLE.'" Online,
http://mikepence.house.gov/index.php?option=com_content&task=view&id=3721&Itemid=94

CHAPTER FIVE: Constitutional Cultures and Subcultures
Hamilton, Alexander. The Federalist Papers. Chutchogue, New York, Buccaneer Book, Inc., 1992, p. 3.

Ryden, John E. "All children deserve quality curriculum and schools." American School & University, Overland Park, Kansas, August 2009, Online, http://asumag.com.

About Carnegie, Carnegie Foundation, Palo Alto, California, Online, http://www.carnegiefoundation.org/about-us/about-carnegie.

CHAPTER SIX: Above Compound English's Nomenclature
The English Language Word Clock, Global Language Monitor, Austin, Texas, Online, www.globallanguagemonitor.com.

Keyword: GUI. Wikopedia, The Free Encyclopedia. San Francisco, California, Online, http://en.wikipedia.org/wiki/Graphical_user_interface.

CHAPTER EIGHT: Axiomatic Laws of Nature and Nature's God
Keyword: fish needs a bicycle, "A feminist slogan, suggesting that men are superfluous to women's needs." The Phrase Finder, Meanings and Origins, United Kingdom, Online, http://www.phrases.org.uk/meanings/414150.html.

Natural. (2001). *Random House Webster's Dictionary, Revised Edition.* (479, 4th ed., 1-4) New York: Ballantine Books.

Jay, John. The Federalist Papers. Chutchogue, New York, Buccaneer Book, Inc., 1992, p.7.

Madison, James. The Federalist Papers. Chutchogue, New York, Buccaneer Book, Inc., 1992, p. 46.

Leff, Lisa. "California Gay Marriage Trial to Kick Off." Associated Press,CBS News, San Francisco, California, Online, January 11, 2010, http://www.cbsnews.com/stories/2010/01/11/national/main6080888.shtml.

Banicki, Elizabeth. "Advocacy Groups Lose Prop 8 Records Appeal." Courthouse News Service, San Francisco, California, April 14, 2010, Online, http://www.courthousenews.com/2010/04/14/26405.htm.

Craig, Tim. "D.C. Judge rules against marriage referendum." The Washington Post, Washington, D.C., January 15, 2010, Online, http://www.washingtonpost.com/wp-dyn/content/article/2010/01/14/AR2010011402616.html?nav=emailpage.

Arson. (2001). *Random House Webster's Dictionary, Revised Edition.* (38, 4th ed., 1-4) New York: Ballantine Books.

Coitus. (2001). *Random House Webster's Dictionary, Revised Edition.* (135-6, 4th ed., 1-4) New York: Ballantine Books.

Made in the USA
Charleston, SC
05 September 2010